A PIAGET PRIMER

HOW A CHILD THINKS

REVISED EDITION

Does an adult perceive the world differently from a ten-year-old? From a six-year-old? A three-year-old? An infant?

The contribution of psychologist Jean Piaget has been precisely to define and chart the differing modes of thought and distinctive stages of mental development *that every child goes through* in journeying toward maturity. His theories have grown out of decades of experiments and observations with children. Now at last *A Piaget Primer* makes them easily available to those who seek entry into that most mysterious and fruitful of realms—the private world of a child.

DOROTHY G. SINGER is currently Research Scientist, Department of Psychology, Yale University, and Research Affiliate, Yale Child Study Center. She co-directs the Yale University Family Television Research and Consultation Center and is a Fellow at Morse College at Yale. She has authored over 200 publications in the area of child psychology. Among her numerous books is *The House of Make-Believe*, published by Harvard University Press, 1990, and *Playing for Their Lives: Helping Troubled Children Through Play Therapy*, published in 1993 by The Free Press.

TRACEY A. REVENSON is Associate Professor of Psychology and Director of the Health Psychology Training Program at the Graduate School & University Center, City University of New York. She is editor-in-chief of the journal *Women's Health: Research on Gender, Behavior and Policy*, co-author of *Understanding Rheumatoid Arthritis*, and co-editor of the forthcoming *Handbook of Health Psychology*. Her major research areas are stress and coping, adaptation to chronic illness, social support, and psychosocial aspects of aging.

A PIAGET PRIMER

HOW A
CHILD THINKS

Dorothy G. Singer

&

Tracey A. Revenson

REVISED EDITION

International Universities Press, Inc.
Madison   Connecticut

Hardcover edition printed 1997 by International Universities Press, Inc.

INTERNATIONAL UNIVERSITIES PRESS and IUP (& design) ® are registered trademarks of International Universities Press, Inc.

Library of Congress Cataloging-in-Publication Data

Singer, Dorothy G.
    A Piaget primer : how a child thinks / Dorothy G. Singer & Tracey A. Revenson.
      p. cm.
    Originally published: New York : Plume, 1996. Rev. ed.
    Includes bibliographical references and index.
    ISBN 0-8236-4134-1 (hardcover)
    1. Cognition in children. 2. Child psychology. 3. Piaget, Jean, 1896-   . I. Revenson, Tracey A. II. Title.
[BF723.C5S6 1997]
155.4' 13—dc21   97-6225
                                               CIP

ACKNOWLEDGMENTS
HAROLD AND THE PURPLE CRAYON, by Crockett Johnson. Copyright, 1955, by Crockett Johnson. Used with the permission of Harper and Row, Publishers, Inc.
From THE PHANTOM TOLLBOOTH, by Norton Juster. Copyright © 1961 by Norton Juster. Reprinted by permission of Random House, Inc.
WINNIE-THE-POOH, by A. A. Milne. Copyright, 1926, by E. P. Dutton; renewal © 1954 by A. A. Milne. Reprinted by permission of the publisher, E. P. Dutton.
THE CHILD'S CONCEPTION OF GEOMETRY, by Jean Piaget, Bärbel Inhelder, and Alina Szeminska, translated from the French by E. A. Lunzer, © Routledge and Kegan Paul 1960, Basic Books, Inc., Publishers, New York.
THE LITTLE PRINCE, written and illustrated by Antoine de St. Exupéry. Copyright © 1943, 1971 by Harcourt Brace Jovanovich, Inc. Reprinted and reproduced by permission of the publishers.

Manufactured in the United States of America

To Our Mothers
for their love and inspiration

Acknowledgments

Many people have contributed to the production of this book. Our warm appreciation goes to Sarah Jane Freymann for her perseverance in getting it all started and seeing it through to completion. For their promptness and diligence in typing the manuscript, we extend our thanks to Virginia Hurd, Judith McBride, and Lisa Rosenberg.

John Thornton and Nicholas Bakalar spent many hours reading, discussing, and improving the many drafts of this book. To both we owe a special thanks for their support, patience, and exemplary editorial skills.

We are especially indebted to Morrie Turner, Mell Lazarus, Al Jaffee, and Dik Browne for allowing us to use their cartoons.

As always, Jerome L. Singer has been a constant source of helpful suggestions and encouragement.

T.R. would also like to thank her friends for their love and support, especially Andrea Hellering, Bill Chance, Rick Spalding, Martha McPhee, Jon Levi, and Dorothy Singer, who is that very special kind of teacher.

We would like to thank Deborah Brody, Senior Editor at Dutton, for giving life to this revised edition. Kim Gallelli was helpful in providing us with materials concerning recent debates in Piagetian theory, and David Sells' careful attention to our corrections and additions made our revision task much easier.

Contents

Preface

When Christopher Robin, the child in *Winnie-the-Pooh*, talks to his woodland friends, a donkey, a tiger, an owl, a pig, and a bear, he is engaged in what Jean Piaget has called *animism*, or the attribution of life to inanimate objects. The charm of A. A. Milne's work and his intuitive understanding of child psychology inspired us to interpret Jean Piaget's developmental theory through the use of literary examples.

Jean Piaget is perhaps the leading child psychologist today. He has written over forty volumes and hundreds of articles dealing with the ways in which a child learns to understand the world. Piaget has examined how a child develops play, language, logic, time, space, number concepts. His writing is difficult for the beginning student in psychology, and for this reason, the goal of our book has been to clarify Piaget's theory through the use of examples from children's literature. We think this is an enjoyable way to learn and to appreciate Piaget, since excerpts from children's literature help concretize Piaget's terms and concepts. We have also used cartoons and comic strips to illustrate a point, and to demonstrate how germane Piaget's theory is to everyday phenomena in children's lives.

We enjoyed writing this book. We hope the reader will be inspired to read Piaget's work with a clearer understanding of his theory as a result of this primer. We believe this book should make an excellent supplementary text to be used in conjunction with a major text in developmental psychology, and along with primary source readings in Piaget. Education and psychology students should find this guide helpful. Parents, teachers of nursery school children, and day-care-center workers should find that they too will better understand Piaget as a result of our presentation.

Preface to the Revised Edition

Jean Piaget died in 1980 at the age of eighty-four. Not only did he have a long and productive career, spanning over sixty years, but even during his final years he was developing new theoretical ideas. Nearly three-quarters of a century after the beginning of his work on the origins of intelligence, the Piaget writings remain a touchstone in the field of child development. What is remarkable is that his theories, so controversial in the 1920s when they first appeared, continue to stimulate research and revisions in the present. The continued importance of Piaget's work is evident in a number of ways: the numerous critiques and extensions to his theory; the sheer number of scholarly books and articles based on Piagetian theory; the inclusion of Piaget's concepts in almost all courses in child development; and the vitality of the Jean Piaget Society, an interdisciplinary organization devoted to the study of cognitive processes and their development as well as to keeping Piaget's ideas alive. While other developmental theories, on a smaller scale, share center stage with Piagetian theory, Jean Piaget undoubtedly will be remembered as one of the world's leading psychologists of the twentieth century.

Piaget's writings also remain essential for those individuals who interact with young children: teachers, child care workers, nurses and doctors, and, most importantly, parents. Nearly twenty years ago we wrote this book in order to make Piaget's concepts more "user friendly." Although the constructs are classic, we decided to revise the book in order to reflect the more complex and technology-laden world today's children live in—where personal computers hold a central place both at school and in the home, and where television often reigns supreme. These emerging technologies offer an opportunity and challenge for us to explore how the insights of Jean Piaget will be sustained or modified as children confront and devise strategies for using these new sources of input.

CHAPTER 1

Jean Piaget and His Theory

At the age of eight months, babies playing with a toy will not search for it after it is hidden under a pillow. At eighteen months, however, they will follow the movements of the toy and continue to search for it after it has disappeared from view.

A four-year-old child is shown two identical glasses filled with the same amount of fruit juice. After the juice from one glass has been poured into a taller, thinner glass, the child is asked, "Which has more?" The child points to the tall, thin glass; in his opinion, the amount of juice is equal to its height.

A five-year-old can learn to walk four blocks from her house to her school, but she cannot trace the route she takes with a paper and pencil. A nine-year-old can trace his route, as well as give people directions without referring to his map. A twelve-year-old can do that, and also think about other ways and shortcuts to get to school.

How can these differences be explained? Is the twelve-year-old "smarter" than his nine-year-old counterpart? Do all children exhibit these differences? Why do children think differently at different ages? Why do children think differently from adults? What goes on inside a child's head?

The French writer Antoine de St. Exupéry reflects on these questions in his classic book, *The Little Prince*:

And after some work with a colored pencil I succeeded in making my first drawing. My Drawing Number One. It looked like this:

I showed my masterpiece to the grown-ups, and asked them whether the drawing frightened them.

But they answered: "Frighten? Why should any one be frightened by a hat?"

My drawing was not a picture of a hat. It was a picture of a boa constrictor digesting an elephant. But since the grown-ups were not able to understand it, I made another drawing: I drew the inside of the boa constrictor, so that the grown-ups could see it clearly. They always need to have things explained. My Drawing Number Two looked like this:

The grown-ups' response, this time, was to advise me to lay aside my drawings of boa constrictors, whether from the inside or the outside, and devote myself instead to geography, history, arithmetic and grammar. That is why, at the age of six, I gave up what might have been a magnificent career as a painter. I had been disheartened by the failure of my Drawing Number One and my Drawing Number Two. Grown-ups never understand anything by themselves, and it is tiresome for children to be always and forever explaining things to them.

Among those special adults who understood that Drawing Number One was not a hat but a boa constrictor digesting an elephant was Jean Piaget.

Just as Freud has significantly influenced our understanding of children's personality development and emotional life, so Jean Piaget, the distinguished Swiss psychologist, has made enormous contributions to our understanding of their intellectual development.

His original research ideas have resulted in new insights as to how children think, reason, and perceive the world—all those mental activities that are labeled *cognition.* Piaget was interested in the qualitative, not quantitative, characteristics of development. He was not concerned with how much the child knows, but how he has come to learn it. It does not matter that a child can recite multiplication tables unless he understands the concepts behind addition and multiplication of numbers or quantities.

Unfortunately, Piaget's writings are difficult to approach, even for the advanced student. The sheer volume of published material is overwhelming, amounting to over forty books and hundreds of journal articles. To read all of Piaget in the original would be quite a time-consuming effort. Furthermore, Piaget's writing style is complex. He introduced many new and unfamiliar concepts in his theory, and used many familiar words, such as *conservation* and *egocentrism*, in ways that differ from the usual definitions. Translation from French to English causes further difficulty. The result is a body of work confusing to many students and nearly inaccessible to people in general.

In the late 1950s and 1960s, as English translations of his later books became available, there appeared to be a Piaget revival among American psychologists. In addition, the belief that American education was in crisis forced educators to seek fresh ideas on curriculum planning. Thus, in the late 1960s and early 1970s, a dozen or so books on Piaget's theory and its application in the classroom appeared, many of which are well written, but directed toward the scholar or educator. In our opinion, these books are still too difficult for the beginning student or interested parent.

It is our intent, therefore, to present an introduction to Piaget's theory of cognitive development in clear, understandable, nontechnical language. This book aims for maximum simplicity without diluting Piaget's work. It is intended as a supplement to, and not a substitute for, Piaget's writings. Those readers interested in a particular topic—for instance, moral development or make-believe play—are urged to read Piaget's original writings on the subject.

This book also differs from the other primers and guides in another way. Comic strips and passages from familiar classics of children's literature have been chosen to illustrate major points and clarify complicated concepts. For instance, Lewis Carroll's *Alice's Adventures in Wonderland* has many wonderful examples of children's language, and Charlie Brown and the Peanuts gang epitomize children at the preoperational stage of development.

Not only should beginning education and psychology students find this guide helpful, but parents, nursery and elementary school teachers, and day-care-center workers should also find it useful for understanding Piaget's contributions to the field of child development. No background in psychology is required or expected of the reader—merely the desire to understand how children think. This is a book for everyone who has ever wanted to know why children have imaginary playmates, insist that the night "makes" dreams, or invent their own rules for the games they play.

The Scholar and His Method

Jean Piaget's background was rich and varied; he was described by his longtime collaborator as "by vocation a zoologist, by avocation an epistemologist, and by method a logician."

Born in the university town of Neuchâtel, Switzerland, on August 9, 1896, Jean Piaget developed an early interest in birds, fish, sea shells, and fossils. This interest turned out to be more than a hobby, and he published his first article, at the age of ten, on an albino sparrow he had seen in the park. Piaget's fascination with biology and science continued into adolescence. He spent after-school hours helping the director of the local natural history museum classify objects in the museum's zoology collection, particularly the mollusk exhibit. The fruit of his labors was the publication of over twenty articles on mollusks before the age of twenty-one. Publication of these articles resulted in an offer to become curator of the mollusk collection at the natural history museum in Geneva. Piaget promptly declined this offer because he was still in secondary school.

His godfather, fearing that the boy was becoming too specialized in the biological sciences, introduced Piaget to philosophy. Piaget was fascinated with the writings of Bergson, Kant, and Durkheim, and by the branch of philosophy known as epistemology, or the study of knowledge. The questions "How do we know?" and "How do we think?" were eventually to dominate his research.

After receiving his doctorate in biology from the University of Lausanne—his thesis on mollusks of the Valais region—Piaget sought a position that would combine the disciplines of biology and philosophy. To do this, he turned to the study of developmental psychology. Working in Bleuler's clinic in Zurich, he studied the psychoanalytic theories of Freud and Jung. Here, and later through his clinical work at the Salpêtrière hospital in Paris, he learned clinical interviewing techniques that would form the foundation for his unique research method.

Piaget then spent two years at the Sorbonne in Paris, studying abnormal psychology, epistemology, mathematics, and the history of science. While at the Sorbonne, his first opportunity to tackle the problem of "How do we know?" arrived. Piaget accepted a job at the Alfred Binet laboratory school in Paris, standardizing the French version of a British intelligence test. Testing French schoolchildren, he became fascinated by the incorrect answers they gave to test questions. He noticed similarities in those wrong answers given by children of the same age, and wondered what reasoning processes the children had followed.

Piaget remained at the school to study this, publishing four papers on the subject. Impressed by one of these articles, Dr. Edouard Clarapède, the director of the Institut Jean-Jacques Rousseau in Geneva, offered Piaget the post of director of research at the institute. What he was offering Piaget was the opportunity to begin formal research in children's thought. Thus, the young biologist and philosopher, who had no formal training in psychology, embarked upon the first phase of a career that would span over sixty years.

Piaget's early work (1925–29) contains some of his best-known experiments, many of which will be referred to in later chapters of this book. The conclusions drawn from these experiments fill five volumes: *The Language and Thought of the Child* (1926), *Judgment and Reasoning in the Child* (1928), *The Child's Conception of the World* (1929), *The Child's Conception of Physical Causality* (1930), and *The Moral Judgment of the Child* (1932).

One psychologist has written, "We turn to Piaget for ideas, not for statistics." In his research, Piaget renounced complicated statistical measures in favor of his acute observational abilities. His methodology was based on a technique of free conversation that he developed while at the Binet school. Believing that children's spontaneous comments provide valuable clues to understanding their thinking, he sought a less-structured method for collecting answers to intelligence test questions than a formal test allows. Using a standard question or set of questions as a starting point, he followed the child's train of thought and allowed the questioning to be flexible. If a child was confused, Piaget could repeat or rephrase the question; if a response was incorrect but intriguing, he could pursue the point further. This is not possible with standardized intelligence tests. Piaget was not concerned with whether a child gave the right or wrong answer, but rather what forms of logic and reasoning he used.

The following are two illustrations of the *clinical method*, as Piaget referred to his technique, part of an early experiment on the way children reason.

BARB (5;6)*: Do you ever have dreams?—*Yes, I dreamt I had a hole in my hand.*—Are dreams true?—*No, they are pictures* (images) *we see* (!)—Where do they come from?—*From God.*—Are your eyes open or shut when you dream?—*Shut.*—Could I see your dream?—*No, it would be too far away.*—And your mother?—*Yes, but she lights the light.*—Is the dream in your room or inside you?—*It isn't in me or I shouldn't see it* (!)—And could your mother see it?—*No, she isn't in the bed. Only my little sister sleeps with me.*

ZENG (6;0): Where do dreams come from?—*They come from the night.*—How?—*I don't know.*—What do you mean by "they come from the night"?—*The night makes them.*—Does the dream come by itself?—*No.*—What makes it?—*The night.*—Where is the dream?—*It's made in the room.*—Where does the dream come from?—*From the sky.*—Is the dream made in the sky?—*No.*—Where is it made?—*In the room.*

* In Piaget's recordkeeping, 5;6 means the child is 5 years and 6 months old.

The second phase of Piaget's work (1929–39) focuses on infancy and the beginnings of intelligence. Again, Piaget observed children in natural settings, like the classroom or playground, and not under laboratory conditions. In fact, for most of this research, Piaget studied his own three children, Jacqueline, Lucienne, and Laurent. Like the "baby biographers" of the nineteenth century, most notably Charles Darwin and Bronson Alcott (father of Louisa May Alcott), who kept diaries of what their children wore, ate, said, and learned each day, Piaget and his wife, Valentine Châtenay, a former student, kept detailed records of their children's behavior. For most parents, when a toddler knocks down a set of blocks it means another mess to clean up; for Piaget it was a valuable clue as to how the human mind reasons. He would ask: Did the child knock the blocks down in any particular order? According to size? shape? color? Did he laugh while he was doing it? From such observations, Piaget traced the origins of mental growth through early childhood. Here is a sample observation Piaget made of his daughter Jacqueline:

Observation 144 . . . During her meal, while she [Jacqueline] is seated, she moves a wooden horse to the edge of her table until she lets it fall. She watches it. An hour later she is given a postcard. Jacqueline throws it to the ground many times and looks for it . . . likewise, she systematically pushes a thimble to the edge of the box on which it has been placed and watches it fall. But it is necessary to note, in observing such behavior patterns, that the child has not yet perceived the role of gravity.

During the time that Piaget was studying infant intelligence, he also was a professor and administrator at the University of Geneva. He was appointed assistant director and later co-director of the Institut Jean-Jacques Rousseau. An interest in international affairs led him to become chairman of the Bureau International d'Education, which has since become affiliated with the United Nations Educational Scientific and Cultural Organization (UNESCO).

In the early 1940s, Piaget emphasized in his research the child's acquisition and understanding of mathematical concepts, such as space, time, and numbers. He revised his clinical method for this research, making it less dependent on language and more on tasks. Taking into consideration the fact that young children may not be able to think abstractly or express their thoughts verbally, Piaget supplemented his conversational method with concrete materials, such as flowers, marbles, glasses of juice, or buttons. These materials are placed in front of the child and manipulated by the experimenter or child. For instance, the child is asked to make identical rows of buttons, or put one flower in each vase, or tie a loose knot. Then the experimenter asks questions about the material and what the child has done with it. By observing how the child uses the materials, and the way he describes what he does with them, the experimenter can form conclusions about the child's thinking.

While continuing his research on space, time, numbers, et cetera, Piaget published a comprehensive three-volume work on the problems of genetic epistemology. *Genetic epistemology* combines the study of biological contributions to intelligence with the theoretical study of knowledge. It differs from child psychology in that it takes an interdisciplinary approach to the problem of development through the study of psychology, philosophy, logic, mathematics, biology, and physics, and is also concerned not merely with childhood, but also with development into adulthood. To pursue problems in genetic epistemology, Piaget established the Centre International d'Epistémologie Génétique at the University of Geneva in 1955. Each year, scholars in the various disciplines assemble at the center to work on a specific problem, such as the child's understanding of causality, and to publish a series of monographs outlining their work.

In addition to his scientific work, Piaget collaborated with Etienne Delessert to write a children's book which is based on how children think in the preschool period. A curious mouse who reasons and thinks exactly as children do in Piaget's experiments is the heroine of the story. In 1952, Piaget was appointed Professor of Genetic Psychology at the Sorbonne, the first non-Frenchman to hold such a position since Erasmus in 1530. He received honorary degrees from such universities as Harvard, the Sorbonne, the University of Brussels, and the University of Rio de Janeiro.

While in his eighties, Piaget continued the research, writing, and teaching he had pursued over sixty years. One of his last works, *The*

Grasp of Consciousness, described a variety of clever experiments concerning the physical movements a child needed to perform certain tasks, such as walking on all fours, or which actions were involved in playing tiddledywinks. Up until his death in 1980, Piaget felt that his theory of genetic epistemology was not yet complete; in fact, he considered himself the "chief revisionist of Piaget."

When Piaget's work first appeared, scholars questioned the theoretical interpretations he gave for the counterintuitive observations he made of his own and other children. They also questioned whether he could make such universal generalizations based on the observations of one, two, or three children. Scholars still question some of these interpretations, as newer and more elaborate methods of studying children and their language have produced different interpretations. For example, there have been criticisms concerning Piaget's failure to study biological contributions to changes in cognitive processes.

Recent research also suggests that Piaget's work did not provide as rich an indication of the infant's competencies as is available today. Some current developmental theorists such as Jean Mandler feel that infants are capable of demonstrating perceptual and symbolic activities earlier than Piaget had realized. Mandler reviewed many of the perceptual experiments concerning infants' abilities to determine boundaries of objects, e.g. seeing a cup as separate from a saucer, long before they can manipulate them manually. Infants were observed as able to separate figures from their ground by about three or four months of age. Important work by Andrew Meltzoff and colleges also support Mandler's contention of the earlier development of symbolic thought. They describe how infants as young as a couple of months and even earlier are capable of imitating movements of others without seeing the movement on their own bodies, such as opening and closing of eyes and mouth. Meltzoff also found that nine-month-olds could observe an action on TV on one day and then on a later day direct their behavior accordingly, a phenomenon called "deferred imitation." These findings are in contrast to Piaget's notion that deferred imitation occurs much later in a child, at about eighteen to twenty-four months when object permanency (the notion that an object "out of sight" is "out of mind") is also established.

Other work besides Meltzoff's has found that infants as young as eight months are able to remember an object that was hidden, and how tall it was. Even Piaget recorded that his six-month-old daughter would kick in her crib when exposed to a toy across the room, acting as if she remembered kicking at this toy when it was actually in her crib. Although Piaget classified this as a motor movement, it seems that the infant did recall the way she had played with the toy when it was close to her. According to Mandler, another example of such rudimentary symbolic thought is evidenced by infants who use conventional signs at six or seven months as repeated by their parents who use sign language with them.

There also have been specific criticisms concerning Piaget's theory of causal reasoning. Experimenters in the 1970s and 1980s attempted to demonstrate that children in the preoperational stage of development can understand causation. These researchers state that if a task is sufficiently simplified and if they do not demand verbal explanations, three-year-olds could demonstrate cause and effect. Merry Bullock and Rochel Gelman, for example, carried out a simple experiment with three- and five-year-olds. A marble was dropped into one of two slots in a box. After two seconds, when the marble was out of sight, a Snoopy doll popped out of a hole in the middle of the box. A second marble was then dropped into the other slot, but no further result occurred. The children then were asked to conduct the experiment themselves to make Snoopy appear. Most of the three-year-olds were able to do the task and were usually correct. The five-year-olds were all able to carry out the task. The major difference between the two groups was in their ability to verbally explain what happened. Almost all the five-year-olds could give a verbal explanation relating to cause and effect, while the three-year-olds could give no verbal explanation or said something irrelevant.

Even in the late 1920s, Susan Isaacs, a researcher in England, questioned Piaget's theory. She believed that it was important for any experiment to have sufficient information about a child's background as well as his or her experience with the objects that were used in experiments. In addition, she felt then, as many developmental psychologists do today, that experimenters must systematically vary the way in which they pose problems to young children.

Neo-Piagetians have accepted Piaget's fundamental theories of development, but are constantly refining his assumptions. Some developmentalists are using an information-processing approach. These theorists think of a child in terms of an information processor similar to a digital computer. They tend to think of changes in cognitive reasoning related to changes in a child's brain or "hardware," which then result in a child's "software" or the development of a new strategy for dealing with a problem. Other scholars claim that cognitive development is spiral, not linear, and neo-Piagetians incorporate culture and social context to a much greater extent than Piaget did.

The work of Howard Gardner or Robert Sternberg, both of whom have outlined theories of multiple areas of intelligence, would also be in agreement with Piaget's notion that children learn about the world through their active engagement. These two psychologists assert that there are various forms of intelligence—music, social, mathematical, to name a few. Thus a child who may be an expert in one area may find another to be difficult. The challenge remains for researchers to try and find the underlying logic needed for each specific intellectual domain in order to better understand Piaget's theory of global stages of intelligence.

Even though Piaget's theories have been expanded and to some extent revised by others, the core concepts remain intact. The clever and seemingly simple experiments devised by Piaget are still used by many developmental psychologists. It is important to realize that Piaget was one of the first psychologists to suggest that cognitive development begins at birth. The Piagetian theories still cleave to the indispensable elements of his research program— stages of development, the child's construction of reality through physical interaction with objects and then symbolic representation. Piaget's theory has left a rich legacy, the value of which continues to be extracted.

CHAPTER 2

The Stages
of a Child's Development

Understanding children's intellectual development is necessary for teaching, working with, or just loving children. Many parents and teachers worry about a child's behavior not being normal: Should he be walking now? Why does she cry when she can't finish a puzzle? How come he's doing so well in art but not in arithmetic? Is he normal? What *is* normal?

There are no definitive answers to these questions. Yet there are guidelines based on observed consistencies among children. These guidelines can serve as a framework in which to view a child's intellectual progress.

Development is a biological term referring to physical growth over time. Applied to psychology, development involves the growth of an individual's thinking, emotions, and strategies for coping with the environment.

Piaget's theory is centered on cognitive development—mental processes such as perceiving, remembering, believing, reasoning. It had little to say about personality development, and discussed emotional behavior in the context of these cognitive processes. According to Piaget, the intellectual abilities that a child possesses at a given age permit certain types of emotional behaviors. For example, a child who has no understanding of what death is or what it means when Grandma dies will not react emotionally in the same way as his older sibling or parents. Thus, the capacity to become an emotional being who is equipped to interact with people depends upon the ability to think, communicate, and understand what's going on.

Piaget's theory, or any theory of cognitive development for that matter, is not in itself adequate to explain human behavior. In fact, there is no single developmental theory which satisfactorily explains behavior. Yet when Piaget's theory is integrated with a developmental theory such as Sigmund Freud's or Erik Erikson's, both of which focus on explanations of personality development and interpersonal relationships, a more comprehensive picture of child development begins to emerge. For example, for an infant to form an emotional attachment to his mother and develop a "basic sense of trust" in her (Erikson's first stage of development), the child must first be able to recognize her mother's face and know that it is the same person who fed her the day before. The mental processes of perception, recognition, and memory are all involved in forming the emotional attachment. Thus, emotion and cognition are constantly intertwined in development.

Most developmental theorists agree that there are basic similarities in children's behavior at different ages or points in their development. Some theorists see the child acting on his world; others see him as a passive and helpless being. Some view development as a smooth and continuous process; others see it as a series of distinct stages. The philosopher John Locke, among others, believed that a newborn baby's mind is a *tabula rasa*, or blank slate, and that the more writing that is put there, the more intelligent the child becomes. Piaget, however, took the opposing view, and, elaborating on what Jean-Jacques Rousseau wrote, believed that the child plays a very active role in the growth of intelligence. The child learns by doing. The world is not just observed and imitated, but interpreted. Piaget was not influenced by the classical learning theory of Hull and Tolman because "it is based upon rodents rather than children."

Piaget defined intelligence as an individual's ability to cope with the changing world through continuous organization and reorganization of experience. Reasoning is the essence of intelligence, and it is those reasoning processes which Piaget studied in order to discover how we know.

Piaget regarded the child as a philosopher who perceives the world only as he has experienced it. The child is born into egocentrism. The child sees himself as the center of the universe, with everything revolving around him and occurring solely for his pleasure. Children can understand only what they have experienced themselves, and expect adults to see things exactly as they do.

© 1964 United Feature Syndicate, Inc.

Egocentrism

In *The Little Prince*, the aviator complained that his little friend, the Prince, never explained anything to him, such as the Prince's drawing of a sheep inside a box. As far as the Prince was concerned

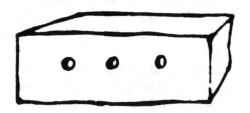

he didn't need a sheep drawn outside of the box; he believed that everyone could see his sheep wandering around inside the box—and could even see it sleeping. By egocentrism, Piaget did not mean selfishness. A child like the Little Prince simply believes that everyone sees the world in exactly the same way he does.

According to Piaget, the mental structures necessary for intellectual development are genetically determined. These mental structures, which include the nervous system and sensory organs, set limits for intellectual functioning at specific ages. As these structures become more developed through maturation, the child can use them more effectively to deal with the environment. A young child has fewer and less-developed mental structures and less experience than the teen-ager or adult. Cognitive development is cumulative; understanding a new experience grows out of what was learned during a previous one.

According to Piaget, *adaptation* is the most important principle of human functioning. Adaptation is the continuous process of using the environment to learn, and learning to adjust to changes in the environment. It is a process of adjustment consisting of two complementary processes, *assimilation* and *accommodation. Assimilation* is the process of taking in new information and fitting it into a preconceived notion about objects or the world.

Just as the one-celled amoeba wraps itself around a piece of food to digest it, the child incorporates new experiences into his cognitive framework or mental set. If a baby has developed the notion of grasping or sucking the breast or bottle, she will do the same with any other object placed before her, such as a rattle or puppet. The rattle and puppet now become part of her experience, and she will be able to recognize them in the future—i.e., *assimilation.*

The twin process, *accommodation*, means adjusting to new experiences or objects by revising the old plan to fit the new information. Initially, a child attempts to understand a new experience by applying old solutions (assimilation); when this doesn't work the child is forced to change his existing conception of the world in order to interpret the experience. The infant who tries to drink milk from his rattle (assimilation) soon learns that rattles only make noise. The rattle is no longer a substitute for feeding (accommodation).

The dual process of assimilation-accommodation

This dual process, assimilation-accommodation, which leads to adaptation, enables the child to form what Piaget called a *schema* (pl. *schemata*).* A schema is a simple mental image or pattern of action, a form of organizing information that a person uses to interpret the things she sees, hears, smells, and touches. For example, the remembrance of a smell can bring back the image of the object associated with the smell, such as a cup of cocoa or freshly baked bread. The child who rides her own bicycle can transfer this action to ride any bicycle because her schema of bike-riding involves a specific pattern of muscle movements and balance. Later, when language skills begin to develop, a word such as "dog" can conjure up a schema of a four-footed, barking animal. A schema organizes perceptions and behaviors in the same way a desk organizer files supplies.

In the cartoon opposite, for Linus, some small objects can be easily bent. Using this schema, he experiments with crackers. After repeated attempts to bend the crackers (assimilation), he finds they cannot be bent—they only break. Linus must revise his former way of thinking about crackers and develop a new schema or mental image concerning them (accommodation). His new schema is that crackers do not bend. This schema has added to his knowledge about the world, and when confronted with similar situations— cookies, crackers, or even other breakable materials, such as parts of toys—he will not try to bend them.

When the great flood comes, Winnie-the-Pooh must get from his treehouse to Christopher Robin's house, but he can't swim. Pooh adapts: "If a bottle can float, then a jar can float, and if a jar floats, I can sit on top of it, if it's a very big jar." Naming it the Floating Bear, Pooh jumps into the water after the jar.

> For a little while Pooh and the Floating Bear were uncertain as to which of them was meant to be on top, but after trying one or two different positions, they settled down with the Floating Bear underneath and Pooh triumphantly astride it, paddling vigorously with his feet.

Pooh first assimilates the jar into his schema or mental set of floating objects, and then must accommodate to it as a float. Because of his

* A difficult term, used in many different senses by Piaget. See the glossary for a definition.

limited experience and overwhelming curiosity, the young child often distorts information to fit his schema, rather than changing the schema. This accounts for some of the strange perceptions that children have. But eventually the child will have to accommodate to the new information in order to adapt.

Adaptation is a process of seeking an equilibrium between the self and the environment. This equilibrium, or *equilibration* as Piaget refers to it, is a balance between the processes of assimilation and accommodation. If a child attains equilibration, then what stimulates him to act and to question?

Piaget identified four overarching elements that guide development: emotions, maturation, experience, and social interaction. All four components work together in guiding development and creating enough disequilibrium to motivate learning. Emotions create the feelings that motivate and excite learning. Maturation is the physical growth process. Through differentiation of the nervous system, mental structures develop and the child becomes capable of great understanding. Experience is a major catalyst because it is only through exposure to a variety of experiences that children can make discoveries for themselves. Social interactions with other people— especially parents, teachers, and other children—provide those experiences as well as feedback. It is important to remember that these four components work together synergistically; for example, the child's mental structures must be developed enough to be able to understand and assimilate the information she is given by parents.

Piaget used the concept of stages to explain his theory of intelligence. He conceived of development as a sequence of stages unfolding over time, stages through which all children pass in order to achieve an adult level of intellectual functioning. Later stages evolve from and are built on earlier ones. The sequence of stages is fixed and unchangeable. No stage can be skipped, and all children pass through the stages in the same order, although children may go through them at different rates. The way that babies and children interact with their world moves them from one stage of development to another.

At each stage the child acquires more complex motor skills and cognitive abilities. Though different behaviors characterize different stages, the transition between stages is gradual. Unlike the magical boy whom Milo encounters in his journey in *The Phantom Tollbooth*, a child moves between stages so subtly that he is scarcely aware of new perspectives.

> Milo turned around and found himself staring at two very neatly polished brown shoes, for standing directly in front of him . . . was another boy just about his age, whose feet were easily three feet above the ground. . . .
>
> "Well," said the boy, "in my family everyone is born in the air, with his head at exactly the height it's going to be when he's an adult, and then we all grow toward the ground."
>
> [Milo said] "In my family we all start on the ground and grow up, and we never know how far until we actually get there."
>
> "What a silly system," the boy laughed. "Then your head keeps changing its height and you always see things in a different way? Why, when you're fifteen things won't look at all they way they did when you were ten, and at twenty everything will change again."

During a transitional period, a child may be in one stage regarding language and in the next one regarding mathematical concepts. What is important is not the age at which each child arrives at a particular stage but the fact that the stages follow an unvarying sequence. All children must be able to understand the world in concrete terms before they can begin to think in the abstract. For example, toddlers will call all four-legged animals "doggie" before they learn that some are cows, horses, or cats.

The age limits for each stage are not absolute, and a child is not retarded or abnormal if at the prescribed age she is not exhibiting a specific behavior. The ages given are average ages and will vary widely. Just as babies may learn to walk at anywhere from ten to eighteen months, so a child can acquire language skills as early as age one or as late as age four.

Stages have played a major role in Piaget's model of development. However, in his later years he wrote that psychologists have relied too much on the notion of stage. More recently, the stage concept has been given less focus in his theory and the characterization of the stages themselves has undergone some change.

First, Piaget recognized that both experience and culture influence the age at which a child will reach a certain level. He observed that schoolchildren in the Swiss countryside reached each stage approximately two years after their Geneva counterparts. Yet all the children passed through the same sequence of stages. This finding has been duplicated in many cultures, including non-Western cultures such as China and Aden. Children will not walk, talk, or learn multiplication tables until they are ready to do so, no matter how much incentive they are given. That is not to say that a parent or teacher cannot encourage a child to develop certain cognitive skills; the child, however, must be physically and psychologically ready to learn.

Second, Piaget recognized that development was fundamentally constant, independent of acceleration or delays due to the child's experience and social context. By describing qualitative changes in children's thinking or speech, their development is made to look more discontinuous than it really is. Robbie Case has used the image of a spiral—the flattening of the spiral at different levels suggests continuous development "flattened" at different levels. The issue of a smooth developmental flow vs. discontinuous (noticeable) changes remains an issue of debate among scholars, though interpreters of Piaget (as well as Piaget himself in his later years) still consider the concept of stages as essential to his theories.

Within each stage there are concomitant developmental changes in the areas of play, language, morality, space, time, and number. We will deal with each of these areas separately, showing the changes from stage to stage. As the emphasis in this book is on the preschool child, the first two stages of development will be discussed in detail in the next chapter, but all four stages will be summarized here to give the reader an overview of cognitive development.

Sensory-Motor Stage:
Ages Birth Through Two

A newborn baby manifests only innate reflex behaviors, such as grasping, sucking, and random movement of the arms and legs. She does not really think: she reacts. Intelligence is first displayed when these reflex movements become more refined. The baby now reaches for and grasps her favorite toy, and sucks on a nipple and not a pacifier when she's hungry.

The child's understanding of the world involves only perceptions and objects with which he has had direct experience. Actions discovered first by accident are repeated and applied to new situations to obtain the same results. If an infant wants a mobile that is dangling above his crib, he will repeat the actions of visually searching for it and grasping it until these actions are coordinated into a plan.

Toward the end of the sensory-motor stage, the ability to form primitive mental images develops as the infant acquires *object permanence*. Up to that time, an infant doesn't realize that objects can exist apart from herself. If a six-month-old baby is shown a toy which is then hidden under a pillow, she will not search for it. At eighteen to twenty-four months, however, the child can understand that even though she can't see the hidden object, it still exists. She knows that when her mother leaves the room she still exists and will reappear.

Preoperational Stage: Ages Two Through Seven

The child in the preoperational stage is not yet able to think logically. With the acquisition of language, the child is able to represent the world through mental images and symbols, but in this stage, these symbols depend on his own perception and his intuition. The preoperational child is completely egocentric. Although he is beginning to take a greater interest in the objects and people around him, he sees them from only one point of view: his own. This stage could be labeled the "age of curiosity"; preschoolers are always questioning and investigating new things. Since they know the world only from their limited experience, they make up explanations when they don't have one. Children's beliefs that natural phenomena are manmade and that everything has life are ways in which they create explanations for confusing experiences.

It is during the preoperational stage that children's thought differs most from that of adults. This difference is explained by St. Exupery's Little Prince.

> If I have told you these details about the asteroid and made a note of its number for you, it is on account of grown-ups and their ways. Grown-ups love figures. When you tell them that you have made a new friend, they never ask you any questions about essential matters. They never say to you, "What does his voice sound like? What game does he love best? Does he collect butterflies?" Instead, they demand: "How old is he? How many brothers has he? How much does he weigh? How much money does his father make?" Only from these figures do they think they have learned anything about him.

Stage of Concrete Operations: Ages Seven Through Eleven

The adult preoccupation with numbers and amounts described above by the Little Prince now surfaces. The stage of concrete operations begins when the child is able to perform mental operations. Piaget defines a mental operation as an interiorized action, an action performed in the mind. Mental operations permit the child to think about actions that were previously performed physically. The preoperational child could count by rote from one to ten, but the actual understanding that "one" stands for "one object" only appears in the stage of concrete operations. In the cartoon on the facing page, the character Wellington is at the preoperational stage because he must count on his fingers. When he reaches the stage of concrete operations he will be able to add, subtract, multiply, and divide in his head—mittens or no mittens.

The primary characteristic of concrete operational thought is its *reversibility*. The child can mentally reverse the direction of her thought. She knows that something that can be added can be subtracted. She can trace her route to school and then follow it back home, or picture where she has left a toy without a hit-or-miss exploration of the entire house. A child at this stage is able to do simple mathematical operations. Operations are labeled "concrete"

The preoperational child

because they are applied only to those objects which are physically present. In the next stage, the child will be able to perform operations on abstract concepts or objects that aren't present.

Children at the stage of concrete operations can classify objects by some characteristic, such as color, shape or size. They recognize that there are hierarchies of classes, and that some classes are really parts of larger classes. An operational child can also mentally arrange objects along some quantitative dimension, such as size or weight. This is known as *seriation*. Whereas a preoperational child

Reversibility

would put sticks in size order by picking them up and comparing them one by one, the operational child can take one look at the whole group of sticks and instantly arrange them in order.

Conservation is considered the major acquisition of the concrete operational stage. Piaget defines conservation as the ability to see that objects or quantities remain the same despite a change in their physical appearance. Children learn to conserve such quantities as number, substance (mass), area, weight, and volume, though not all concepts are achieved at the same time. Let's look at one of Piaget's classic experiments on the conservation of volume. A child is shown

two identical glasses of juice and asked "which has more." Both the child in the preoperational stage and the child at the stage of concrete operations will answer that the two are identical. Then the experimenter pours the juice from one of the glasses into another glass— this time, a taller, thinner glass—and the child is asked again,

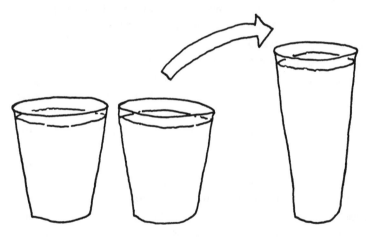

"Which has more?" The preoperational child will invariably point to the taller, thinner glass. She believes that it contains more juice because the juice level is higher. The concrete operational child, however, has learned to conserve, and understands that although the heights of the juice in the two glasses are different, no juice has been added or subtracted. She understands that the size or shape of the container doesn't determine the amount of juice it contains.

Stage of Formal Operations: Ages Eleven Through Sixteen

The child in the concrete operational stage deals with the present, the here and now; the child who can use formal operational thought can think about the future, the abstract, the hypothetical. Piaget's final stage coincides with the beginning of adolescence, and marks the start of abstract thought and deductive reasoning. Thought is more flexible, rational, and systematic. The individual can now conceive all the possible ways a problem might be solved, and can look at a problem from several points of view. The adolescent searches for a solution in a systematic fashion. Although he claims he lacks brains, the Scarecrow in *The Wizard of Oz* is able to reason in such a deductive manner. When faced with the problem of crossing a huge mountain crevice he reasons, "We cannot fly, that is certain; neither can we climb down into this great ditch. Therefore, if we cannot jump over it, we must stop where we are."

The adolescent can think about thoughts and "operate on operations," not just concrete objects. He can think about such abstract concepts as space and time. He develops an inner value system and a sense of moral judgment. He now has the necessary "mental tools" for living his life.

Piaget hypothesized that no new mental structures emerge after formal operational thought, and that intellectual development consists solely of an increase in depth of understanding. One critique of Piagetian theory is that it does not capture the cognitive development that occurs after formal operations is reached. For example, as Hans Furth has pointed out, Piaget's theory does not deal directly with social cognition or creativity, leaving open questions of whether there might be a period or stage beyond formal operations. Most scholars, however, doubt the existence of such a stage, suggesting that one can still use general Piagetian principles to understand these domains of knowledge.

CHAPTER 3

How Intelligence Develops

For Piaget, intelligence meant exploring the environment. It may be in the form of a baby pushing, pulling, and tasting a toy, or later in the form of an adult's thinking as he classifies, sorts, matches, and integrates information. Both the child and the adult are transforming objects and attempting to make sense out of the environment through the two processes we discussed in the previous chapter—assimilation and accommodation. Piaget viewed intelligence as an equilibrium between these two processes. When assimilation outweighs accommodation, as in a child's game where materials are used to represent objects that are not present (a stick becomes a doll, a piece of clay is a cookie), *thought is egocentric and highly personal.* When accommodation prevails over assimilation, when a child faithfully reproduces the movements of objects or persons (clapping hands, drinking from a cup), *thought is imitation.* Cognitive behavior requires a balance between these two functions of assimilation and accommodation.

The growth of intelligence occurs through the four main stages that we have sketched briefly in Chapter 2: Sensory-Motor, Preoperational, Concrete Operations, and Formal Operations. Now we will discuss the first two stages more fully. Some children may develop certain intellectual capacities more readily than others, but all children go through these progressive stages. Sequences of behavior, both internal and external, that a child develops are called *schemata.* These schemata, or plans, are the repeated patterns of behavior you may see in a child's daily repertoire, such as the continuous reaching for and grasping of a rattle, the search for the bottle's nipple, the kicking of a mobile hanging over a crib, the game of "Peek-a-Boo." These patterns of behavior develop by trial and error. The random movements of the baby gradually become more purposeful so that he can adapt to the environment. As children learn more complex ways of responding, and as they develop more complex schemata, they move gradually to a higher stage of intellectual development.

I. Sensory-Motor Stage: Ages Birth Through Two

Within this first period of the infant's life there are six substages:

1: Random and reflex actions (0–1 month)
2: Primary circular reactions (1–4 months)
3: Secondary circular reactions (4–8 months)
4: Coordination of secondary schemata (8–12 months)
5: Tertiary circular reactions (12–18 months)
6: Invention of new means through mental combinations
   (18 months–2 years)

Substage 1: Random and reflex actions (0–1 month). The infant is born with certain reflexes such as sucking, grasping, crying, vocalizing. All of his initial movements are random, disorganized, and uncoordinated, and appear to have no purpose. Gradually, the baby gains control. He makes constant attempts at accommodation to the environment when he is awake. For example, an infant's sucking begins to take on a pattern. The rooting or searching behavior of the newborn moves to a systematic pattern of sucking at the nipple only when he is hungry. The baby may suck his own finger, or even his parent's finger, as a pacifier, but will reject it if he is hungry. Sucking acts vary; the baby may want the nipple only when he is hungry. He may suck the edge of the quilt to calm himself, or he may even suck a rattle in a playful mood. In this first month of life, repetition of these acts or schemata form the beginnings of intellectual development. The baby described in the following passages from *The Door of Life* by Enid Bagnold exemplifies Substage 1.

The baby was four days old. Now he would come in the dawn, regally in the midwife's arms, already expectant. He fed greedily at one breast, and as his mother passed him over her body in the darkness to the other, he snuffled in a passion of impatience, learning already that there was a second meal, seizing the nipple, choking, and sinking into hardworking silence. Sensory exploration, which in the peril of his first day on earth had centered only in his lips, now spread to his limbs; and his hand, as he worked, from lying stiff like a star, began to move, travelling over the squire's silk night dress, scratching the silk with his nail in a flurry of his fingers, trying the linen sheet, learning the textures. . . . All his power was in his lips. His hands were fronds, convolvulus tendrils catching at surfaces, but only half informed.

Substage 2: Primary circular reactions (1–4 months). The baby now begins to discriminate among shapes and forms. She smiles at some objects and gazes at others for longer periods of time. For example, she knows what her bottle is. Images, such as the hood of the bassinet, dangling toys, or her parent's face, are now examined with sustained interest. A baby may stare curiously at her own hands and not realize they are her own.

The bassinet hood that formerly had no particular meaning for the baby now becomes an object that is assimilated into the baby's schema. A circular reaction takes place because the baby looks to see an object, is pleased when it appears, and then keeps looking. The baby, however, at this stage believes that when an object is removed from his sight the object no longer exists. He has not learned that objects, space, and time can exist apart from himself. Thus, when the bottle falls from the sleepy baby's grasp, he begins to cry. He does not realize that the bottle exists near his body, in the folds of the blanket. He waves his arms frantically and cries, but he does not search for the lost object. Not until he is older, at about eight months, will "out of sight" no longer mean "out of mind." The eight-month-old will search for his lost object.

Substage 3: Secondary circular reactions (4–8 months). The schemata or strategies that the baby has developed now become more complex and repetitive. The infant looks at an object in order to act. Thus, seeing and hearing develop into sharper discriminations. Where previously the baby followed a light with her eyes, or smiled at a familiar face, she can now look at an unfamiliar object for a longer time. The baby imitates more complex actions and repeats sounds that are new to her.

New sights and sounds are woven into the baby's schemata through the process of imitation. The activities of the baby are mainly rediscoveries and not inventions of new acts nor applications of the known to new circumstances. For example, Piaget described his daughter Jacqueline at four months, watching her hand as it moved toward her face. Her hand moved toward her nose and finally hit her in the eye. She was frightened by this, unaware that the object of fright was her own hand. Similarly, Winnie-the-Pooh makes some footprints in newly fallen snow and is completely unaware that the tracks are his. He walks in circles and believes he has found the pawmarks of a Wozzle! When a parent dangles a rattle over the baby's crib, the baby's whole body wriggles with delight. But the baby in the early months of this stage does not reach up toward the rattle. He is unaware that his hand is an extension of himself. If the parent, however, places the rattle in the baby's hand, he will grasp it tightly. He does not yet know that he has the power to reach out for the rattle. Coordination between vision and grasping into an integrated schema does not yet exist.

Substage 4: Coordination of secondary schemata (8–12 months). This stage marks the beginning of what is called *intentional behavior.* The baby is determined to reach an object he desires. Piaget described his son Laurent's persistent efforts to reach a matchbox that Piaget had hidden behind a cushion. At nine months, Laurent pushed Papa Piaget's hand away and pulled at the object with his other hand. Not only were Laurent's movements intentional, but they were a means to an end. Laurent persevered until he obtained the desired object.

In *Silas Marner* we have an excellent description of intentional behavior:

> The infant's eyes were caught by a bright glancing light on the white ground, and with the ready transition of infancy, it was immediately absorbed in watching the bright living thing running to-

ward it, yet never arriving. That bright living thing must be caught, and in an instant, the child had slipped on all fours, and held out one little hand to catch the gleam. But the gleam would not be caught in that way and now the head was held up to see where the cunning gleam came from. It came from a very bright place; and the little one rising on its legs toddled through the snow, the old grimy shawl in which it was wrapped trailing behind . . . toddled on to the open door of Silas Marner's cottage and right up to the warm hearth.

The notion of *object permanency* is now part of the child's intellectual repertoire. Two separate ideas become joined or coordinated. One schema is the awareness that the object exists independent of the self, the other, that the infant is capable of searching for it. Most babies enjoy the game of "Peek-a-Boo." The baby's face lights up with joy when mother's face reappears from behind the cushion or from behind her hands. The baby watches with intense interest and anticipation. The reappearance of her face confirms the baby's notion that he has about her "permanency" and her ability to come back again.

In *The House at Pooh Corner*, Pooh drops a fir-cone by accident into a brook and believes it has disappeared. As he lies resting near the stream, he spots his fir-cone floating by on the other side of the bridge. Pooh thinks this is strange, and wonders if he drops *another* fir-cone into the water whether that one will reappear. Pooh repeats his act and is delighted with each fir-cone's reappearance. He is testing out the notion of object permanency.

Symbolic meaning also develops in this fourth stage. A baby can retain images of objects in her head even when the object is not present. For instance, a baby smiles when she hears the nursery door being opened. She anticipates the appearance of her mother before she enters the room. Piaget's daughter Jacqueline could discriminate between the sounds of a spoon tapped against a glass or against a bowl as a signal that mother was going to offer her a particular food. The sound of the spoon against the bowl signified food that she did not like, and she clamped her mouth shut.

At this stage the child responds in order to produce a desired result, and he will respond similarly in a new situation. Sometimes he is successful in repeating his act; sometimes the outcome is disaster. This kind of "intent" often appears funny to adults, such as when an infant attempts to repeat an act which seems appropriate to him. A one-year-old who puts a hat on his head may at some later time turn a sand pail upside down and put it on his head, too.

Substage 5: Tertiary circular reactions (12–18 months). Increased exploration now begins to take place. Until this time, intelligence consisted of applying familiar information to new situations. But now the infant, confronted with a situation in which her old schemata do not work, must invent a new plan. This is the period when toddlers explore the mysteries of the videotape recorder or play with nesting blocks and toys of various shapes and sizes, trying to fit things together and pull things apart. When a baby in this period tries to reach outside of her playpen for an object wider than the spaces between the bars, she learns to tilt the object after some trial and error.

A baby discovers, too, at this stage that he can let things drop out of his grasp intentionally. Thus, the baby who drops food on the floor during mealtimes is doing several fascinating things. First, he can control the dropping of the food by himself; second, the food falls through the air and he can watch its flight; and third, he can vary where he drops the food so that he can scatter the pieces all around the high chair. The baby has learned new ways of performing the same act. In the same fashion, Winnie-the-Pooh, playing beside the stream, soon varied his schemata by dropping various sizes of fir-cones into the water.

Substage 6: Invention of new means through mental combinations (18 months–2 years). The actions of groping and exploring that characterized the earlier months begin to diminish, and the infant starts to think about an action *before* she acts. Because the toddler has carried on so many "experiments" in the previous stage, she can now use some of the information she has assimilated to perform new acts without the trial and error that dominated her earlier months. Gestures as well as limited speech help a child indicate that she is thinking about a solution to a problem. A classic example comes from Piaget's own notes about his daughter Lucienne. When Piaget gave Lucienne a box with a chain tucked inside it, she attempted to retrieve it but was not successful because the opening was too small for her hand to fit inside. Lucienne opened and closed her mouth in an attempt to signify that the box needed a wider opening. Piaget called this opening of the mouth a motor indicator or symbol that represented the box and its opening. This imitation of the box helped Lucienne to formulate a plan. Indeed, she then put her finger in the box, enlarged the slit and retrieved the chain. Imitation in the form of a motor signifier marks the way for the beginnings of thought, and the movement into the next main developmental stage.

II. Preoperational Stage: Ages Two through Seven

This period is called "preoperational" because the child still has not developed the mental structures needed for logical or abstract thought. The child is still dependent upon what he sees, and his reasoning is without systematic or logical processes.

The preoperational period is divided into two substages, the Preconceptual (ages two to four years) and the Perceptual or Intuitive Thought Period (ages four to seven years). In the Preconceptual stage the child begins to use language and mental images, and attempts to generalize in illogical ways. In the Period of Intuitive Thought, problem-solving depends on instinctive thought and appearances, not on judgment or reasoning. Piaget called this kind of thinking in children transduction or *transductive reasoning*: Reasoning from a particular idea to a particular idea without logically connecting them. The child believes that simultaneous occurrences necessarily have a cause-effect relationship. Reasoning is inconsistent; distortions of thought are common.

Syncretic thought is one form of transductive reasoning. For example, Piaget reported his daughter Jacqueline's conversation when she was ill and wanted oranges. Piaget told her that oranges were still green and not yet ripe. Later as Jacqueline drank her camomile tea, she said, "Camomile isn't green, it's yellow already. . . . Give me some oranges!" The child's reasoning made sense to her. If tea is yellow, then oranges must be yellow at this time, too. Jacqueline attempted to link two separate bits of information together and the result was egocentric, faulty, prelogical reasoning. In *Winnie-the-Pooh*, Pooh has just been bitten by a bee in his search for honey. As a result, he decides they are "the wrong sort of bees," and therefore "would make the wrong sort of honey." Pooh's reasoning is egocentric, transductive, and syncretic.

At times, preoperational children reason in a way that Piaget labeled *juxtaposition reasoning*; a child concentrates on details and parts of an object and does not relate the parts to the whole. For example, when Piaget asked a five-year-old child to put together objects that were alike, the child placed a woman next to a fir tree, a bench against a house, and coupled a church with a small tree and a motorcycle. The juxtaposition of these collections was arbitrary. Similarly, a child may reason that a large sailboat floats because it is heavy, a small sailboat floats because it is light, a leaf floats because it is thin, paper floats because it is flat. The child does not grasp the underlying notion that explains the phenomenon of floating. He reasons without generalizing or forming a logical concept.

Egocentric behavior is probably the most striking characteristic of the preoperational child. Egocentrism is manifested in a child's constant use of questions and through the child's persistent monologues, whereby she keeps a running chatter going even though no one may listen. Indeed, the child in this period believes that everyone feels and thinks as she does. Pooh's first monologue in *Winnie-the-Pooh* is an excellent example of egocentrism. Pooh hears a buzzing noise in the forest and immediately believes that buzzing noises means that bees are about, and that bees only buzz to make honey, and of course "the only reason for making honey is so *I* can eat it."

Children in this period believe in *animism*, the notion that inanimate objects are alive. Christopher Robin, for example, attributes life to his stuffed animals. There is Piglet, a weak and timid pig; Eeyore, the cynical, pessimistic donkey; Owl, all wise and knowing; Rabbit, mean and clever; Kanga, the bossy, practical symbol for motherhood; and of course, Roo, the mischievous baby. In *The Wizard of Oz*, we find Dorothy befriending a Tin Man and a Scarecrow. Children enjoy these stories because they accept the idea that they can attribute life to their toys and talk to them. Piaget asked many children whether inanimate objects such as wind, rivers, clouds, and the sun were alive. He found that below the age of seven, children ascribed life to these forces of nature.

Children in this period also believe that natural phenomena are man-made. Piaget termed this belief *artificialism.* Children believe that human beings created lakes, mountains, trees, the sun, and the moon.

In *The Phantom Tollbooth*, Milo, the young boy, meets Chroma, the conductor of colors:

"You don't listen to this concert—you watch it. Now, pay attention."
    As the conductor waved his arms, he molded the air like handfuls of soft clay, and the musicians carefully followed his every direction.
    "What are they playing?" asked Tock. . . .
    "The sunset, of course. They play it every evening, about this time."
    "They do?" said Milo quizzically.
    "Naturally," answered Alec; "and they also play morning, noon, and night, when, of course, it's morning, noon, or night. Why there

© 1968 United Feature Syndicate, Inc.

Artificialism

wouldn't be any color in the world unless they played it. Each instrument plays a different one . . . and depending, of course, on what season it is and how the weather's to be, the conductor chooses his score and directs the day."

In *The Wizard of Oz*, The Scarecrow, Tin Woodsman, and Cowardly Lion all exhibit artificialism: They believe that the Wizard of Oz will be able to give them brains, a heart, and courage—even when the Wizard is exposed by Toto the dog as an ordinary man.

The preschooler is constantly questioning and investigating new things. The child knows the world only from her own experience. If she can't find an explanation for something, she'll make one up. The magic rituals children believe in (getting the wishbone of the chicken, not stepping on sidewalk cracks) are attempts to control a world which doesn't make very much sense. Children sing chants such as "Rain, rain, go away, come again another day," thinking they can control the elements.

The preoperational child believes in the realism of words. Names exist as part of the object named. In *Winnie-the-Pooh*, Rabbit says that the North Pole is "sure to be a pole because of calling it a pole, and if it's a pole, well, I should think it would be sticking in the ground, shouldn't you, because there'd be nowhere else to stick it." During the expedition to the North Pole, Baby Roo falls into the water and Pooh saves him with a long pole he happens to find. Christopher Robin proclaims that the expedition is over and that Pooh has found the "North Pole."

Pooh also uses language quite literally. Pooh lived in the forest all by himself "under the name 'Sanders.' " Christopher interprets this to mean that there must be a sign hanging above the door with the name "Sanders" printed on it.

Children in the preoperational period also use onomatopoeia, or words that sound like noises that objects make. Children say "choo-choo" and "bow-wow" long before they say train or dog. Pooh received his name through onomatopoeia. While hunting for honey in one of his adventures, he held on to a balloon for a long period of time as he floated in the air toward the beehive. Since he tried to hold tightly to the string of the balloon, he was unable to use his hands to chase away the flies. Whenever one landed on his nose, Pooh had to blow it off by saying "Pooh." And that is how he got his name.

The preoperational child takes metaphors and figurative expressions in the literal sense. In *Charlie and the Chocolate Factory*, the factory's owner, Mr. Willy Wonka, takes the children on a tour:

> STOREROOM NUMBER 71   WHIPS OF ALL SHAPES AND SIZES
>
> "Whips!" cried Veruca Salt. "What on earth do you use whips for?"
> "For whipping cream, of course," said Mr. Wonka.
> "How can you whip cream without whips? Whipped cream isn't whipped cream at all unless it's been whipped with whips. Just as a poached egg isn't a poached egg unless it's been stolen from the woods in the dead of the night!"

Another major characteristic of preoperational intelligence is the concept of *centering*. By this Piaget means that a child can see an object only in relation to its particular function, or can focus on only one aspect of the object at a time. In *Winnie-the-Pooh*, the donkey Eeyore is the unfortunate victim of centering. He loses his most compelling feature, his tail. Pooh promises to help look for the missing tail. Visiting Owl, Pooh notices that the bell-rope on Owl's door looks rather familiar to him.

> "Handsome bell-rope, isn't it?" said Owl. Pooh nodded.
> "It reminds me of something," he said, "but I can't think what. Where did you get it?"

Owl describes how he found it hanging over a bush. Owl thought someone must live in the bush, so he rang it, but nothing happened. He rang it again and it came off in his hands. Since nobody wanted the bell-rope, Owl took it home and hung it on his door. For Owl, a tail without Eeyore attached to it is not a tail; hanging over a bush it becomes a bell-rope.

The preoperational child has not yet acquired conservation. That is, he does not understand that objects or quantities remain the same despite a change in physical appearance. Eeyore the donkey has not yet learned to conserve. Piglet plans to give Eeyore a large red balloon for his birthday. On the way there, Piglet falls down and the balloon bursts. All that is left is a "small piece of damp rag." Nevertheless, Piglet is determined to give the present to Eeyore.

"Eeyore, I brought you a balloon."
"Balloon?" said Eeyore . . . "one of those big coloured things you blow up?" . . .
"Yes . . . but I fell down . . . and I burst the balloon."
"My birthday balloon?"
"Yes, Eeyore," said Piglet, sniffing a little. "Here it is. With—with many happy returns of the day."
"Thank you, Piglet," said Eeyore. "You don't mind my asking," he went on, "but what colour was this balloon when it—when it *was* a balloon?"

Poor Eeyore cannot understand that red remains red even when the balloon is small and no longer round and full.

The child who has acquired conservation of volume understands that the amount of juice in a tall, thin glass does not change when it is poured into a short, fat one. In an experiment on conservation of substance, Piaget presented a child with two identical balls of clay and then elongated or flattened one of them right before the child's eyes. He then asked the child if the two pieces both had the same amount of clay. The preoperational child will say "no," believing that the experimenter has actually produced more clay by changing the shape of it. This can be attributed to the child's tendency to focus on only one aspect of a given object at a time. The child considers "length" or "height," but not the two simultaneously. A child who is in the concrete operational stage, however, can conserve matter, and understands that although the shapes of the two pieces of clay are different, no clay has been added or subtracted. This child understands that the two dimensions, "height" and "length," are related.

A four- or five-year-old has difficulty placing objects in a series. When asked to line up sticks of unequal lengths according to their size, the preschooler is bound to mix up the order and place longer sticks before shorter ones. She goes through much trial and error until she succeeds. The young child also experiences considerable confusion concerning relationships, whether between objects or people.

For example, young children classify objects inaccurately. A child in the preoperational stage often thinks that taller people are older and shorter people are younger; he uses height as the basis for his reasoning. It is amusing, too, when a child is asked about his brother. He may admit that he has a brother, but he is unable to understand that he too is a brother, an example of the lack of reversibility.

Finally, children's intellectual growth in the preoperational period is influenced by their play. Play is important in the development of intelligence. The symbolism or the representation of absent objects by substitute objects is one way in which a child learns about the world. When a child uses a mud pie to represent cake, or makes

Assimilation-accommodation in make-believe play

building blocks into a gasoline station, she is attempting to assimilate information about the environment into existing schemata. Through the continuous interaction of assimilation and accommodation, the child gradually gains some sense about objects and their purposes. For example, when Pooh uses his umbrella turned upside down as a boat, he is assimilating information about boats and umbrellas, accommodating the umbrella to his image of boats, and adapting to a new situation in which a vehicle is needed to help him sail home in the flood.

The youngsters in the cartoon on page 39 are playing "space man" using a box for their rocket ship. Through assimilation-accommodation, they are adapting to the schema of a ship about to take off. Mother represents reality for them, and they cleverly work her into the game as "Mission Control."

The growth of intelligence is nurtured by make-believe play, as this is the primary means the child has for assimilating the reality of the world into existing experience. In this preoperational period much of the child's learning about language, morality, time, and numbers will take place through play. As children mature, they will move into the next stage, *concrete operations*. Here, they will begin to classify objects correctly, conserve, use socialized language, relinquish their animistic notions, and generally view the world in a more logical way.

CHAPTER 4

Playing and Imitating

Listen to the noises in a nursery and you'll hear a proud new mother or father make sounds like "goo-goo" or "itsy-bitsy baby." You may even see raised eyebrows on mother's face, weird contortions of mouth and cheeks, and you'll hear lots of giggling. What you're observing is a perfectly normal scene of parents engaging in "play" with their newborn babies. Play starts at birth, according to Piaget. Through numerous observations of his own three children in their nursery, and later in their toddler, preschool, and school-age periods, Piaget formulated his theory of play.

Play begins as imitation. In the early stage of the infant's life, in the sensory-motor period, the baby's play is predominantly a copy of the sounds and actions of the persons or animals in his environment. Gradually, these imitations evolve into the three main forms of play that Piaget has labeled *practice play*, *symbolic play*, and *games with rules*. Before we discuss these three stages of play, let us examine what Piaget meant.

Imitation

Babies use their mouths, eyes, hands, and feet in imitative "functional pleasure" games. Within this early infant period, from birth to about twenty-four months, Piaget described six substages of play, each one evolving from the previous one and becoming more complex and organized. Imitation is nearly pure accommodation. The infant simply copies an act he sees without necessarily understanding the movements. For example, a mother may wave "bye-bye" to the infant. The infant imitates the movements with his hands, but may not fully understand the words. As a matter of fact, he may even wave "bye-bye" to someone who enters a room. Only later does the baby understand the words, and when he plays with his toys he can make believe he is going away, or a doll is going away, and the doll can wave bye-bye in the appropriate manner. When the child plays at this level, utilizing a reality symbol in his own game, it is assimilation. When the baby imitates you as you wash your face, he is accommodating to the environment, but later, when he can wash his doll's face in a make-believe sink, he is assimilating his information about washing into a little game that may not always reflect the real world. For example, a doll may be washed with a pretend cloth made out of scrap material, and soap may be a piece of cardboard.

There are six substages in this period of *imitation* that involve the infant's gradual movement from purely reflex behavior to a more complex imitation of models. As the child grows and develops, she learns to copy sounds and gestures without the extensive trial and error that characterized her early months.

In Substage 1, the baby merely acts with his reflexes—sucking, crying, responding to a loud noise by a startle, moving his head toward light, grasping his own fingers or another's fingers. Gradually, these reflex movements become more purposeful. The sounds of one baby can trigger the cries of all the babies in the nursery. This crying is attributed to the inability of a baby to distinguish between his *own* cry and that of a nearby baby. Thus, the crying of other babies stimulates the vocal reflex and has a contagious effect. The external stimulus, the sounds coming from another baby, causes the crying. But soon imitation begins. A baby cries when he hears another baby crying, but when the baby stops, he stops too.

In Substage 2, the baby repeats what someone has done, assimilating the action into her own schema as though it were her own. For example, if his baby daughter Jacqueline made "la" or "le" sounds, she could imitate Papa Piaget's sounds if indeed they were "la" or "le" sounds. But Jacqueline would not imitate a new sound that was not *first* emitted by her.

In Substage 3, true imitation of sounds and movements begins. Thus Jacqueline now imitates sounds and movements that Papa made even if she had not previously made that sound or movement herself. The movements that a baby imitates must be movements that she can see on her own body, such as hand or leg movements. For example, in this stage a baby could not imitate a facial expression because she is unable to *see* her own face.

In Substage 4, the child's repertoire of sounds and movements expands to include sounds that are new to her and movements or imitations of facial expressions of others. Piaget described this as follows:

> At 0;8, Jacqueline was moving her lips as she bit on her jaws. I did the same thing and she stopped and watched me attentively. When I stopped, she began again. I imitated her, she again stopped, and so it went on.

This imitation of movements initiated by the infant, but that the infant *cannot see on her own body*, marks an important step in the imitation process. From imitation of mouth movements, the infant can then begin to imitate other facial movements and become aware that parts of other faces, such as nose, eyes, ears, and cheeks, are also like her own features. Thus, if a mother were to raise her eyebrows and puff out her cheeks to make a "funny face," her baby could now imitate this expression in a playful way.

In Substage 5, the infant continues to imitate the adult's voice and attempts to form words and imitate more complex movements. The infant is more flexible and his imitation now is actually a question of *degree* when compared to the previous stage. No new forms of imitation appear, but experimentation with existing sounds and gestures increases, and the child is more persistent. Imitation here becomes a systematic accommodation. The child seems to perform acts over and over, and the beginnings of ritual-like behavior appear.

Finally, the infant, at about eighteen months, enters Substage 6. Now he can copy more complex behavior without the trial and error of the previous stages. The baby also can imitate nonhuman objects, such as his pet dog or cat, as well as objects that are not present.

This imitation that begins toward the end of the second year of life is called *symbolic imitation*, because the baby uses something other than the original object to symbolize the object. Piaget's daughter used a walnut to substitute for a cat. As she moved the walnut along the edge of a big box she made "meow, meow" sounds indicating that, indeed, the walnut was her cat and the box, the garden wall. Here then, with Jacqueline's little game, is the beginning of the world of make-believe.

Practice Games

When a child swings on a swing for the sheer pleasure of the movement, he is engaged in *practice* or *mastery play*. Much of a child's play is just for the pleasure of the senses—feeling, touching, movement of arms, legs, toes, or fingers. The job of swinging on a rope swing just for this sensory-motor pleasure is experienced by Avery, a boy in E. B. White's classic book, *Charlotte's Web*.

> "Then you straddled the knot, so that it acted as a seat. Then you got up all your nerve, took a deep breath and jumped. For a second you seemed to be falling to the barn floor below, but then suddenly the rope would begin to catch you, and you would sail through the barn door going a mile a minute, with the wind whistling in your eyes and ears and hair."

Some sensory-motor play involves tasting, smelling, or even listening to sounds. Thus, sense modalities and motor movements may be involved at different times in a child's enjoyment of a game.

When Linus plays with a rubber band in the cartoon on page 46, his fingers and hands are involved in a practice game. The pleasure of finally mastering his movements outweighs the initial frustrations of the trial and error that preceded mastery.

In *Trio for Three Gentle Voices* by Harold Brodkey, we find Faith, in the toddler stage, playing with five spoons.

> She could get two spoons in each hand and a fifth in her mouth. She stood up and walked away. . . . She toppled to the floor and lay on

her back, idly she kicked her heels, "Otsee wah-wah," she said. "Otsee poosfah." She sat up and put two spoons down the front of her overalls. She took two more spoons in her left hand and the last one in her right hand. She rolled over until she was on all fours; it was the only way she could rise. Then she stood up. She glided toward the kitchen, leaning slightly to one side, perhaps because the spoons inside her overalls tickled.

This play has no purpose other than that of sensation. The humming of Winnie-the-Pooh as he exercises before his glass and simply plays with sounds such as "Tra-la-la" or "Rum-tum-tickle" are examples of sensory-motor play with song. The sounds are made merely for the pleasure they bring, despite the meaninglessness of each syllable. Adults engage in sensory-motor or practice play as well. For example, we all enjoy trickling sand through our fingers.

Ritualistic play, or play that is later called practice play, begins in the sensory-motor stage and is a form of mastery. The child repeats an act to see if it will recur, as well as for the pleasure it gives him. For example, Eeyore the donkey dropped a balloon into an empty pot over and over just for the pleasure of the act. Baby Roo practiced jumping into the sand. He kept jumping and falling into mouse-holes. He would climb out of them and jump in a hole again. Baby Roo played this game repeatedly, just as Eeyore played his balloon game. Wilbur the pig, in *Charlotte's Web*, rolled in the manure or the hay or scratched his back against the fence because it felt good. A baby kicks a mobile hanging over his crib over and over and squeals with delight each time it moves. These forms of play are not yet true games but pleasurable acts in themselves that eventually emerge into more complex forms of play.

In *The House at Pooh Corner*, "Poohsticks" begins as a sensory-motor or practice game and evolves into a more complex game with rules. At first Pooh dropped a fir-cone over the side of a bridge and leaned over to watch it reappear on the other side. Then he dropped *two* fir-cones into the water and waited to see which fir-cone would come into sight first. It was difficult for Pooh to distinguish between the two cones and name a winner since they were the same size. He then used one big and one small fir-cone in his game. Pooh and his

Practice play—sensory motor skills

animal friends substituted sticks for fir-cones "because they were easier to mark." Thus a game that began as a practice game, one that initially was played for enjoyment of the reappearance of the fir-cones, evolved into a game with rules and order. Each stick had a definite size and the winner was the first stick that emerged. The game began with a definite "Go," and involved rules, a score, more than one player, and an eager expectation for the winning stick to reappear!

Symbolic Play

Near the age of two, the swing that was formerly used just for practice and mastery now may become a rocket ship traveling to a distant planet, or a wild bird that flies through the air. It is true that practicing new tricks on the swing may continue through childhood and adolescence, but now another element is introduced into the swing game—that of make-believe, or pretend. *Symbolic games*, or play that distorts reality and implies representation of an absent object, occupies a major period of the child's world from ages two through five years. A child who pretends a box is a car, a pot is a drum, the broom is a wild horse, and a mud pie is a birthday cake is engaged in make-believe or symbolic play.

Piaget used the term "ludic" to describe such symbolic play. Ludic comes from the Latin word *ludus*, meaning game. These pretend games may appear funny or silly to an adult, but they are quite serious to the child. A child may imitate or make believe he is a dog or cat, or he may invent an imaginary playmate that accompanies him all over. The child who does this is able to differentiate between what is real and what is fantasy. The use of pretend and make-believe helps him to make this differentiation. In his play he rehearses his life experiences, testing them out in varying ways. His imaginary companions and characters later evolve into the adult's fantasy life or daydreams—his private, secret, inner world of make-believe. In symbolic play, commonplace materials are often substituted for the real objects. In *Winnie-the-Pooh*, Christopher Robin and Pooh are caught in the "Terrible Flood." They desperately need a boat large enough for two. Pooh, who is a "Bear of Very Little Brain," said something "so clever that Christopher Robin could only look at him with mouth open and eyes staring": "We might go in your umbrella." Christopher Robin realized how clever this was of Pooh, and turned the umbrella upside down and they both were able to get in. " 'I shall call this boat The Brain of Pooh,' said Christopher Robin, and The Brain of Pooh set sail forthwith in a southwesterly direction, revolving gracefully."

It is not unusual to see preschoolers involved in *parallel play*. Just watch some children sitting in a sandbox or playing in the doll corner. Each one is busy with her own toys, playing in her own fashion and interacting with her neighbor only in a perfunctory way. But if one child were to leave the sandbox or the doll corner, her friends would become disconsolate. The conversations in the sandbox may be in the form of monologues—each child talking to herself about her own particular plan of action, and each child possibly making her own rules. Yet each one enjoys the presence of her friends.

Some children engage in what Piaget called *compensatory play*. If a child has been spanked, he may then spank his doll or scold his teddy bear. If a child witnesses an unpleasant act or has a frightening experience, he may then symbolically play this out. Piaget believed this compensation or catharsis enabled a child to dissociate the unpleasant act from its context, and then assimilate it into his behavior. For example:

> At 3;0, Jacqueline was impressed by the sight of a dead duck which had been plucked and put on the kitchen table. The next day I found J. lying motionless on the sofa in my study, her arms pressed against her body and her legs bent: "What are you doing, J.?—Have you a pain?—Are you ill?" "No, I'm the dead duck."

Play therapists, professionals who work with children who have emotional disturbances, use materials such as dolls, sandboxes, and paints in their playrooms. Because children may not be able to communicate their feelings through words, the trained therapist interprets their play. Some of a child's concerns and apprehensions might be revealed as a child plays. Piaget made a distinction between primary symbolism (conscious assimilation, conscious pretend play) and secondary symbolism or unconscious assimilation. When Jacqueline used her walnut shell to represent a cat (in an example cited earlier), she was quite aware of her actions. Sometimes, a child uses toys to express concerns of which he is unaware. Piaget used the example of a child who is jealous of his baby brother. When playing with two dolls, the child may make the smaller doll go away on a long trip while the bigger doll remains home, safe with mother. The child in this game may not consciously be aware of his desire to get rid of baby brother. This is secondary symbolism or play that is compensatory.

Another example of compensation is found in *A High Wind in Jamaica* by Richard Hughes. A group of children are held captive on a ship. Rachel, who is about six, plays "house" constantly. One reason she perseveres in this type of game is to relieve her loneliness and the fact that she misses her parents. Another reason is for her own inner joy of pretending.

> She was never happy unless surrounded by the full paraphernalia of a household: she left houses and families wherever she went. She collected bits of oakum and the moultings of a worn out mop, wrapped them in rags and put them to sleep in every nook and cranny. . . . She could even summon up maternal feelings for a marline-spike and would sit up aloft rocking it in her arms and crooning. . . . Further there was hardly an article of ships' use from the windlass to the bosun's chair, but she had metamorphosed it into some sort of furniture, a table or a bed or a lamp or a tea set: and marked it as her property.

Secondary symbolism, or play that deals with unconscious symbols, falls into three groups: symbols relating to the body; symbols relating to elementary family feelings such as love, jealousy, and aggression; and symbols relating to anxieties about birth of babies. Piaget also posited that there is an analogy between dreams and the games of children, but with one difference. In dreams, nightmares may appear, but when a child plays a game, he can control the fear, and even make it funny or enjoyable. A child we know played "alligator" over and over in an attempt to master his fear of the animal. The game was played with much vigor and laughter as he, the "alligator," pretended to swallow a toy or the arm of his mother. The game helped to ease his fears, so that gradually this game appeared less and less in his play activities.

Games with Rules

According to Piaget, *practice play* begins within the first months of a baby's life and *symbolic play* begins about the second year. *Games with rules* rarely occur before ages four to seven and belong mainly to the stage of concrete operations, ages seven to eleven. *Games with rules* remain with an individual throughout his life and develop even more fully as the person matures. Piaget called games with rules "the ludic activity of the socialized being." Symbolic games in the form of daydreams or fantasies continue throughout one's life. Practice games or sensory-motor play may continue in forms such as sifting sand through one's hands, floating in a pool, practicing a tennis serve against a wall, or playing "air guitar."

Games with rules do make up a large segment of a child's play from seven to eleven, but the preschooler may also engage in games with simple rules. Rules are either handed down or spontaneous, and as the Miss Peach cartoon, below, illustrates, may be quite elaborate!

© 1957 New York Herald Tribune, Inc.

Preschooler's games with rules

Some games are what Piaget called "institutional." These are the games that seem to be passed down from generation to generation such as "Take a Giant Step," "Hide and Seek," and "Hop-Scotch."

Younger children generally learn these games by imitating older siblings or other children in the neighborhood. The symbolic games that children play may evolve into games with rules, just as the practice games of "Poohsticks" evolved into a game with rules. Piaget described a game played by shepherd boys of Valais, who used branches from a hazel tree to be their pretend "cows." The branches were Y-shaped so that the tips of the Y were horns and the lower part of the Y was the body. Eventually the game became more elaborate and the "cows" fought one another. Soon rules were developed about the conditions of fighting such as pushing, jerking, pulling, and the rules evolved into who could "win" a "cow." In just this way children have evolved elaborate games from the symbolic play of cops and robbers, cowboys and Indians, or even doll play. Once rules are made, then games that were purely sensory-motor combinations or symbolic games become games with rules. Games with rules involve competition, a code that is institutionalized, or a code that may be a temporary, spontaneous agreement.

Let us look at our swing for a moment. The swing that was used for practice and mastery, and later as a rocket ship or a wild bird, may also become a swing game with rules. The children may compete to see who swings highest, there may be rules for taking turns, or there may be rules concerning the limitations (no zigzag swinging or over-the-bar swinging).

In *Alice's Adventures in Wonderland*, the Queen's game of croquet is an example of games with rules. "Croquet balls were live hedgehogs and mallets live flamingoes, and the soldiers had to double themselves up and stand on their hands and feet, to make the arches." The rules were temporary and spontaneous and violated the institutionalized code. The game was played by the caprices of the Queen, much to the annoyance of Alice, who was at about age seven, when rules are considered important. Alice is annoyed, too, at the Caucus Race since this game had no beginning or end. The players simply ran in a circle and everyone was a winner.

Games with rules become the adult's world of play. Intellectual games of chess, checkers, bridge, and sports involve rules that are accepted by all. As children leave the world of make-believe, private fantasies become the adult's symbolic games. The growing, maturing child who maintains this "playful attitude" has a better chance of growing into the imaginative, creative adult.

Purpose of Play

Now that we have looked at Piaget's theory of play, some questions may arise. Why should children play? Is it necessary? Is it a waste of time? Is play innate? Can we teach a child to play?

Play constitutes a major part of a preschooler's life and is a valuable aspect of the child's cognitive, social, and emotional development. As we examine the numerous benefits of play, we will see that the adult personality may very well have its foundation in the play of the child.

We have found in our research that play can be taught. In a series of experiments with preschoolers, children have been taught how to play imaginatively through the use of modeling. When an adult shows a child a new way to use materials, or suggests a theme or story line to a child, this may be all that is needed by the child to start her own imaginative game. An adult who is playful with a child is also sanctioning the normal play that some children may feel reluctant to engage in for fear of laughter or ridicule by their peers. We believe that all children have the capacity for symbolic or make-believe play, and we accept Piaget's premise that play is one developmental aspect of a child's personality. We feel, too, that parents need to set the scene for play by encouraging children to explore new materials, to use their bodies in a more relaxed way, to use all of their senses. We believe that parents can help children express their emotions through play. For example, the use of puppets engaged in a simple story about a child's fears or jealousies can allow a child to express these feelings through the voices and actions of the puppet show. *Mister Rogers' Neighborhood* on television uses puppets in a make-believe town to deal with jealousy, partings, sickness, sharing. In just this way, parents can utilize a few props to help children talk about their worries as they play. This technique is only one facet of play and, as we have seen, Piaget's notion of compensatory play deals with this. We have found in our research that children who are engaged in make-believe play are more lively and smile more than children who wander aimlessly around the nursery school room, or who engage in aggressive acts.

Sensory-motor play, practice play, symbolic play, and games with rules all have their particular benefits. The infant who plays with her rattle or kicks her mobile as it swings over the crib is learning about her world. She begins to anticipate movement of the mobile, but learns that she must initiate the movement herself. The sense of touch enables her to keep the mobile in motion and she masters this schema. Taste, hearing, touching, and seeing, all enrich the child's play. Her mastery of games enables her to become more competent as she explores the world. Each time she succeeds in throwing a ball, riding a bicycle, or pumping the swing, the child feels more effective and more competent. The make-believe games that involve some mastery of skills eventually become more elaborate and may incorporate rules and order. Thus play may be a combination of any of the stages we have described.

Each form of play has distinct benefits. For example, practice play or mastery play enables a child to improve his motor skills. Games with rules teach the child to share and wait his turn, to learn a sense of order and logic, and to accept either the winner's or the loser's position with appropriate reactions. Games of make-believe may involve sensory-motor skills, some rules and order, and of course, sharing, turn-taking, and even delay of gratification. For example, if a child plays tea-party, he learns to set a table, to go through the motions of making the tea and pouring it "without spilling" the water, while the "guests" await their turn. All the children can touch, taste, and smell the "tea," and even listen to the teapot whistle on the toy electric stove. Baking cookies in the sandbox encourages the sensory-motor play of early childhood such as the pleasure of touching the mud and water or the rolling of the mud pie. The game becomes more advanced into make-believe as children take the roles of baker and customers. Even in this symbolic game, rules may appear about who plays each role, how much mud is used for each pie, or which trucks are to be used for delivery. Later, in more elaborate board games, or street games, not only are motor skills developed (finger dexterity in the former, and gross motor skills such as running, jumping, skipping, hopping developed in the latter), but definite rules are set down and the child learns to take his turn, how to compete fairly, keep score, and share the materials of the game.

Let us look now at some specific benefits that accrue from play:

When children use a variety of materials in their play, they can learn to *sharpen their senses*. The infant's chewing on the rattle for sensory-motor pleasure or rubbing a piece of soft material for tactile pleasure evolves into more elaborate forms of play. Children learning to swim enjoy the sensations of water and the pull against gravity. Riding a bicycle gives one a sense of balance, and a child can feel the wind in her face as she rides with even moderate speed. Smelling flowers, fruits or vegetables; touching velvet, pine cones, or rocks; listening to a clock tick, water trickling, leaves crunching; looking at colors, shapes, and objects such as a drop of water peered at under a magnifying glass—all of these experiences can be enhanced through play. Some crunchy leaves in a toy cereal dish make a pretend breakfast. Water with food-coloring makes a cup of chocolate. Scraps of silk or velvet feel soft on a doll's bed, and small rocks and pebbles of various colors and shapes become the "gold" in a pirate's treasure box.

Vocabulary grows as children play mastery games in which words are needed, for example, to express "higher" when one climbs or swings or throws a ball. Words that involve complexities about a board game or game of cards begin to emerge in a child's vocabulary. One child we know who learned chess at the age of four years has not only learned the names of the pieces but also has developed his spatial relationship ability to an advanced degree. As children play make-believe games they need more expressive terms to symbolize the range of objects and places they need to enhance their pretend play. Playing a game of pirate requires a child to name such objects as map, gold, island, ship.

Concentration is increased when a child engages in play whether it be practice, symbolic, or games with rules. Sticking with the ball-game until one learns to throw the ball into the hoop, or to make contact with the bat, or learning to catch the jacks as the little ball goes into the air, forces the child to concentrate and persist. In make-believe play the enjoyment of the game prevents distraction and keeps the child involved for a long period. The development of concentration will benefit the child later in school as he attends to his lessons.

Flexibility is found among children who engage in play. With practice play, a rope or tire may serve as a swing, or a stick as a bat. Children can climb rocks when there are no climbing gyms. They can slide down grassy hills when no wooden slides are available, and assemble a skateboard with a roller skate and a board. In make-believe games, children learn how to substitute objects for the ones they do not have. We have seen children make "snowballs" out of mud pies by covering them with the white fluffy seeds of dandelions. Round cereal boxes make wonderful drums, and children can become orchestra conductors when they hold a "baton" made from a paper-towel spool.

Play creates an atmosphere of *harmony*. As children play with each other, they learn to share the toys, the bicycles, the balls and bats, and how to respect each other's toys and materials. In practice games, one must wait a turn for the swing or slide. In games with rules, each child has a specific turn to play. This does not mean that children who play won't have fights or arguments, but certainly as children engage in games with each other, socialization begins.

When children play, they learn how to *delay gratification*. In practice games or games with rules, children learn to wait for their turn, and in make-believe games a child can say to another, "Wait, I'm making your supper. It will be ready soon," or "We have to sail to the treasure island in our boat, then we'll look for the pirate's gold." Children rehearse the messages they hear from adults concerning the need to be patient and to wait. Practice play, symbolic games, or games with rules reinforce these waiting or delaying capacities. Later, in school this capacity for delay will prove important.

Playing different roles such as a teacher, storekeeper, astronaut, doctor, bus driver, explorer, or parent helps a child "try on" these occupations or roles and learn about society in miniature. Children enjoy dressing up and pretending that they are different people. In this way they begin to think about their future and the variety of roles that people have in this world.

Empathy can develop, too, as a child learns to play the role of another person. She can begin to understand how someone feels when he is sad or happy. By playing house, for example, children begin to see how earnest mothers or fathers are when they want their children to obey them, or how happy they are when the "child" in the pretend game does something that pleases the "Mommy."

Finally, make-believe play leads to an *expansion of a child's imagination and creativity*. More than practice play, more than games with rules, symbolic play enables children to use images, to see events in their minds, to imitate sounds and voices and movements that belong to other people or animals. A child invents new ways of using materials and objects. He can be anyone, go anywhere, do anything in his imagination. When a child learns to pretend, he learns to master his environment. He also learns to distinguish between what is reality and what is fantasy. When one develops imagination, one can work out alternate plans for problem-solving and rehearse in one's mind ways to reach a goal.

Adults can continue to play—and they do. Not only do they continue sensory-motor games, practice games, and games with rules, but they continue symbolic play through storytelling, writing, and participating in amateur theatricals. All adults can continue symbolic play by keeping their imaginations active and allowing the fanciful to enter their thoughts. We have stated that the imaginative child is a smiling child. She laughs more and appears more lively and spontaneous than the child who engages in routine tasks or only in motor-skill games. We contend that the adults who use their imagination appear to have more satisfying inner lives and more inner resources to ward off boredom.

The play life of children can continue throughout adulthood if they find pleasure in their activities and approval from their parents. The role of a parent can be to set an atmosphere conducive to play by supplying simple materials, and by sharing even for a few minutes a day in the child's make-believe games. The parent must also learn when to withdraw from the game, and must be willing to allow the child his own manner and style. There is mutual pleasure when the child's imaginative growth leads to the parents' delight in watching imagination and creativity unfold.

CHAPTER 5

How Language Develops

If you've ever eavesdropped on a group of preschoolers while they are busily at play in a sandbox, or watched a youngster when she is alone in her room with only a favorite teddy bear, then you know that children have a language of their own. They may use words familiar to the adult ear, but more often than not, they have a completely different meaning in mind. The young child doesn't talk only to people, but to her toys, to the trees, to herself. She speaks in non sequiturs, and rarely keeps to a topic for more than two sentences at a time.

Piaget's first book, *The Language and Thought of the Child*, published in 1926, dealt with such questions as why children speak in the first place, and whether they understand each other when they converse. Underlying language acquisition are elementary logic and reasoning processes. Piaget began his research in this area by observing two six-year-old boys at the Maison des Petits (the preschool attached to the Institut Jean-Jacques Rousseau) for a month. Without interfering in their play or other activities, he sat in a corner of the schoolroom, recording all their remarks and conversations. Analyzing these observations, Piaget discovered that children's speech can be divided into two basic types—*egocentric speech* and *socialized speech*. Each type serves a very different function. We assume that the purpose of most speech is communication between people, but this is not always the case with children's speech.

Egocentric Speech

A child first begins to use speech at ages two to four. Language in its beginning stages is completely egocentric. The child's speech reflects what he's thinking at the present moment, regardless of whether what is being said makes sense to anyone but himself. When he speaks, he is oblivious to who may or may not be listening. Speaking is a pleasurable sensory-motor experience in itself.

The most basic form of egocentric speech is repetition or *echolalia*. As described earlier, a child in the sensory-motor stage repeats a simple motion, such as hitting a mobile above the crib, for two reasons: to assimilate the action into her schema, and to give herself pleasure. A child just starting to speak repeats sounds and words for the same two reasons. She babbles because she enjoys listening to herself make sounds. At this stage, most children don't have the slightest idea what they're saying or what it means. This babbling often accompanies an activity, such as playing with hand puppets or watching the pet cat. The child is so absorbed in the activity that she repeats nonsense syllables or elementary words (ta-ta-ta-ta or kitty-kitty-kitty) without being aware she's making sounds at all.

Youngsters also repeat what they hear others say, thinking what they've said is original. For example, one boy will turn to his friend and say, "Let's play cowboys and Indians!"; his friend immediately replies, "Let's play cowboys and Indians!" Interestingly enough, this type of verbal repetition can occur hours, days, or even weeks later! This is called *delayed echolalia*. We've all heard stories of a youngster repeating to a total stranger some potentially embarrassing remark he's overheard his parents say in private.

Children can often be heard giving lengthy soliloquies on such varied subjects as birthday presents, Barbie dolls, Batman, or their kindergarten teacher without anyone being in sight. As in theater jargon, Piaget called this type of speech a *monologue*. Whether a child is alone or in the middle of a group of children, he talks to himself, about himself, for himself. He is oblivious to any listeners.

© 1961 United Feature Syndicate, Inc.

Monologue—a form of egocentric speech

Skipping from one thought to another with no logical connection is common in the speech of preschoolers. As illustrated in the Peanuts comic strip above, a young child speaking a monologue is either unaware of the listener, or doesn't care whether or not someone is listening. Frieda talks to no one in particular half the time, and she leaves in the middle of a sentence without even finishing her thought or saying goodbye.

Children talking to themselves is an accepted, everyday occurrence. Yet, if we see an adult waiting for a bus and talking to himself, it's another matter altogether. An adult's "thinking aloud," though, is very similar to a child's monologue. Some psychologists postulate that an adult's thought process is another form of speech called inner speech and that thinking actually consists of talking to oneself without saying anything aloud. Children's egocentric monologues may very well be the basis of adult thought and reasoning.

Collective monologue, the most socialized of the three forms of egocentric speech, consists of simultaneous monologues: two or more children are all talking together, none of them listening to or responding to any of the others. Often, children play alongside one another, but are completely absorbed in their own fantasies and conversation. The child pays little attention to questions asked by his playmates: he gives "answers" that are unrelated to specific questions. At this stage, each child doesn't even try to understand or listen to anyone else's point of view.

There is a good illustration of collective monologue in *Winnie-the-Pooh*. Christopher Robin gives a party to celebrate Pooh's heroics in saving Piglet from the flood. All the forest animals are invited and are seated at a long wooden table, each involved in his own thoughts or conversation.

> "Hallo, Eeyore!" said Roo.
>
> Eeyore nodded gloomily at him. "It will rain soon, you see if it doesn't," he said.
>
> Roo looked to see if it didn't, and it didn't, so he said, "Hallo, Owl!"—and Owl said "Hallo, my little fellow," in a kindly way, and went on telling Christopher Robin about an accident which had nearly happened to a friend of his whom Christopher Robin didn't know, and Kanga said to Roo, "Drink up your milk first, dear, and talk afterwards." . . .
>
> "H—hup!" said Roo accidentally.
>
> "Roo, dear!" said Kanga reproachfully.
>
> "Was it me?" asked Roo, a little surprised.
>
> "What's Eeyore talking about?" Piglet whispered to Pooh.
>
> "I don't know," said Pooh rather dolefully.
>
> "I thought this was *your* party."
>
> "I thought it was *once*. But I suppose it isn't."
>
> "I'd sooner it was yours than Eeyore's," said Piglet.
>
> "So would I," said Pooh.
>
> "H—hup!" said Roo again.

Collective monologues may be centered around one general topic, as when they are all watching Pooh open his present, or can be

Collective monologue

totally unrelated. Roo is steadily hiccuping, Kanga is scolding him, Eeyore is complaining, and Owl is talking to Christopher Robin about a person Christopher Robin doesn't even know. All the animals are happy to be together at the party, but each egocentric animal is involved with his own thoughts.

Socialized Speech

Why, then, at the age of about seven, does a child's use of language become less egocentric and more socialized? Piaget hypothesized that before that age the child has little need to communicate clearly. Everyone makes an effort to understand him. A baby cries and her mother runs to feed or change her. A toddler yells and her babysitter brings her a toy. A schoolchild knows that someone will be there to meet her at the bus stop. But, as children grow older and begin to have contact with other children as egocentric as themselves, they have to demand attention to be heard and understood. Socialized speech patterns begin to appear at age five or six, at about the same time children enter elementary school. It is a time for more play with others, sharing toys, and cooperation in group situations.

Though calling it socialized speech implies communication with others, the speech of six- or seven-year-olds is still very egocentric. Conversations are often one-sided, but there is a noticeable change: The child now pays attention to the speaker and responds to what has been said. There is an exchange of information, a conversation.

Piaget divided socialized speech into four categories: adapted information; criticism; commands, requests and threats; and questions and answers. The first category, *adapted information*, is the basic form of socialized speech. The function of language shifts from being a way of giving oneself pleasure to being a way of exchanging ideas or opinions. Adapted information is the foundation on which conversations are built. A child exchanges thoughts or ideas with others, telling the listener something that will interest him or influence his actions. For instance, one child may tell another which piece is missing from a puzzle so that they can finish it together, or a child may talk about his new puppy as part of "Show and Tell."

Adapted information

Though not completely logical, the following dialogue from *Through the Looking Glass* is a good illustration of adapted information:

"I hope you've got your hair well fastened on?" he [the Knight] continued, as they set off.

"Only in the usual way," Alice said, smiling.

"That's hardly enough," he said, anxiously. "You see the wind is so *very* strong here. It's as strong as soup."

"Have you invented a plan for keeping the hair from being blown off?" Alice enquired.

"Not yet," said the Knight. "But I've got a plan for keeping it from *falling* off."

"I should like to hear it, very much."

"First you take an upright stick," said the Knight. "Then you make your hair creep up it, like a fruit tree. Now the reason hair falls off is because it hangs *down*—things never fall *upwards*, you know. It's a plan of my own invention. You may try it if you like."

Such a conversation is communicative in nature. By asking questions, Alice shows a genuine interest in the Knight's ideas. At age seven and a half, Alice is becoming less egocentric in her thought and language.

Piaget found that *criticism*, the second category of socialized speech, occurred frequently in the speech of preoperational children. Their criticism is intentional and directed toward a specific person.

In that sense, it is similar to adapted information. The person being criticized, however, is not expected to respond to the criticism. For that reason, Piaget justified classifying criticism and adapted information as different categories of socialized speech. This distinction is a very subtle and often confusing one. Children's criticism is almost always based on anger or emotion and seldom on logic or reason, and is usually directed at others. Criticism is used by children to assert their superiority over others. Humpty Dumpty behaves this way in his first encounter with Alice:

> "Don't stand chattering to yourself like that," Humpty Dumpty said, looking at her for the first time, "but tell me your name and your business."
> "My *name* is Alice, but—"
> "It's a stupid name enough!" Humpty Dumpty interrupted impatiently. "What does it mean?"
> "*Must* a name mean something?" Alice asked doubtfully.
> "Of course it must," Humpty Dumpty said with a short laugh: "*my* name means the shape I am—and a good handsome shape it is, too. With a name like yours, you might be any shape, almost."

Commands, requests, and threats implies a definite interaction between speaker and listener. Through a command, request, or threat, a child attempts to influence the actions of his audience so as to achieve a desired goal. Often this is accompanied by action or intent of action. The Queen of Hearts, in *Alice's Adventures in Wonderland*, has only one way of settling all difficulties: "Off with her head!" Luckily for Alice, this threat was never accompanied by action. At the Mad Tea Party, the Mad Hatter and March Hare issue commands to the Dormouse, "Wake up, Dormouse . . . Tell us a story." Alice is amazed at the fact that all the creatures engage in the use of commands. "Everyone says 'come on!' here," thought Alice. . . . "I never was so ordered about before in all my life, never!"

The final subdivision of socialized speech is *questions and answers*. Children's questions begin as early as age two or three, becoming incessant at the ages of four to six. Now that children have language, they seek answers to everything. Most questions asked by children call for an answer. However, Piaget found that very young children will often ask questions which are addressed to no one in particular and for which no answer is expected. Sometimes, they even answer the questions themselves. As Alice fell down the rabbit-hole, she

> went on saying to herself, in a dreamy sort of way, "Do cats eat bats? Do cats eat bats?" and sometimes, "Do bats eat cats?" for, you see, as she couldn't answer either question, it didn't matter which way she put it.

Children's earliest questions are primarily "what is?" questions, concerned with names and descriptions of people, places and things. The Little Prince is full of these questions:

> Abruptly, without anything to lead up to it, and as if the question had been born of long and silent meditation on his problem, he demanded:
> "A sheep—if it eats little bushes, does it eat flowers too?"
> "A sheep," I answered, "eats anything it finds in its reach."
> "Even flowers that have thorns?"
> "Yes, even flowers that have thorns."
> "Then the thorns—what use are they?"
> I did not know. At that moment I was very busy trying to unscrew a bolt that had got stuck in my engine . . .
> "The thorns—what use are they?"
> The little prince never let go of a question, once he had asked it.

As children enter the second half of the preoperational stage (age five or six), questions become concerned with causality, origins, and the physical world.

Even more than their questions, children's answers supplied Piaget with valuable clues to the development of logic and reasoning. Much of Piaget's early research at Maison des Petits in Geneva consisted of collecting children's spontaneous answers and comparing them for similarities.

Children's answers and explanations usually make sense to no one but themselves. The preoperational child has only a limited amount of knowledge and experience to draw on. There's still a lot he doesn't

© 1962 United Feature Syndicate, Inc.

Questions about causality, origins, and the physical world

know, but that doesn't prevent him from using his imagination and making up explanations, as in the Wee Pals cartoon on the next page.

Because of his egocentric nature the child is unable to recognize or accept anyone else's viewpoint. The child assumes that since everyone thinks exactly as she does, there's no need for explanations. Introducing Pooh, Christopher Robin explains:

"He's Winnie-ther-Pooh. Don't you know what *'ther'* means?"
"Ah, yes, now I do," I said quickly; and I hope you do too, because it is all the explanation you are going to get.

Egocentrism is also behind the preoperational child's tendency to use pronouns without telling what "it" or "he" refers to. Children also tend to leave out important aspects of a story or incorrectly order sequences of events. Events may be related with no apparent connection, as in the cartoon on page 68.

Another common misuse of language is exemplified by the

© 1970, 1971 The Register and Tribune Syndicate, Inc.

Explanations—using imagination

child's confusion in dealing with homophones. In the mouse's story as told to Alice, we recognize several homophones and Lewis Carroll's clever use of them.

> "Mine is a long and sad tale!" said the mouse turning to Alice and sighing. "It is a long tail, certainly," said Alice, looking down with wonder at the Mouse's tail.

In the same sequence, Alice says, " 'You had got the fifth bend, I think?' 'I had *not*!' cried the Mouse, sharply and very angrily. 'A

Egocentric speech

knot!' said Alice, always ready to make herself useful, and looking anxiously about her. 'Oh, do let me help to undo it!' "

As the child moves out of egocentric speech, linguistic play with phonemes and miscellaneous sounds, rhythms, and sing-song games help the child realize the flexibility of speech. Later, practice in punning and joking provides good exercise for vocabulary and also an opportunity to remove a thought from its context and use it in a new way. Learning to make puns and to carry on a joking repartee by remote word associations is the one linguistic activity that helps children to develop verbal skills along with logical and creative thinking. Probably the best example of the use of puns is seen in the Mock Turtle's Story, in which he describes to Alice the type of education he has had.

"I only took the regular course." "What was that?" enquired Alice. "Reeling and Writhing, of course, to begin with," the Mock Turtle replied; "and then the different branches of Arithmetic—Ambition, Distraction, Uglification and Derision." . . . "Well, there was Mystery, . . . ancient and modern, with Seaography: then Drawling . . . Drawling, Stretching, and Fainting in Coils." . . . "And how many hours a day did you do lessons?" . . . "Ten hours the first day . . . nine the next, and so on." "What a curious plan!" exclaimed Alice. "That's the reason they're called lessons, . . . because they lessen from day to day."

Before we leave the subject of language, let's take a closer look at the conversations of children in the period of intuitive thought (ages four through seven)—the time when they are just beginning to use socialized speech. Piaget described six types of conversations: association with the actions of others, collaboration in action, quarreling, primitive argument, collaboration in abstract thought, and genuine argument. The distinctions among these categories are subtle.

In *association with the actions of others*, even though a child might be talking to another about her *own* activities from her *own* point of view (which could be labeled a monologue), she associates what she's saying with the listener. There is no collaboration; that is, the child is still talking only about herself and matters that concern her. But she is aware that someone is listening to what she's saying. The following conversation is a good illustration of *association with the actions of others*:

"Which reminds me—" the White Queen said, looking down and nervously clasping and unclasping her hands, "we had *such* a thunderstorm last Tuesday—I mean one of the last set of Tuesdays, you know."

Alice was puzzled. "In *our* country," she remarked, "there's only one day at a time."

The Red Queen said "That's a poor thin way of doing things. Now *here*, we mostly have days and nights two or three at a time, and sometimes in the winter we take as many as five nights together—for warmth, you know."

"Are five nights warmer than one night, then?" Alice ventured to ask.

"Five times as warm, of course."

"But they should be five times as *cold*, by the same rule—"

"Just so!" cried the Red Queen. "Five times as warm, *and* five times as cold—just as I'm five times as rich as you are, *and* five times as clever!"

Alice sighed and gave it up. "It's exactly like a riddle with no answer!" she thought.

"Humpty Dumpty saw it too," the White Queen went on in a low voice, more as if she were talking to herself. "He came to the door with a corkscrew in his hand—"

This conversation from *Through the Looking Glass* is very close to being a collective monologue. However, the three are talking about a common subject, and are aware of who is listening, but each is concerned with only her own feelings about the subject.

Collaboration in action describes those conversations which connect thought with action. The conversation is centered around an activity being performed by the two speakers, such as building sand castles or setting the table for dinner. In contrast, *collaboration in abstract thought* is a simple discussion of some topic which is not a shared activity. It is the only type of conversation which has a true interchange of thoughts and ideas; there is a collaboration of thought on some mental image, upcoming event, memory or conversational topic which need not depend on some shared physical activity. If two children are at the circus and talking about the clowns parading in front of them it is collaboration in action; if the same children are at home talking about the circus they saw the week before, it is considered collaboration in abstract thought.

Both these types of speech are less egocentric than association with the actions of others.

Quarreling, primitive argument, and *genuine argument* are conversations which express an exchange of information, but in an opposition of opinions and action. Through quarreling, children first express the need to make themselves understood. There is usually no justification for the disagreement; an emotion such as anger or frustration is usually the cause.

Argument begins from the moment when the speakers confine themselves to stating their opinions, instead of teasing, criticizing, or threatening. In primitive argument, the speakers disagree and give explanations for their differing points of view. Of course, in Wonderland it doesn't always make sense:

Alice went timidly up to the door, and knocked.

"There's no sort of use in knocking," said the Footman, "and that for two reasons. First, because I'm on the same side of the door as you are; secondly, because they're making such a noise inside, no one could possibly hear you." And certainly there *was* a most extra-ordinary noise going on within—a constant howling and sneezing, and every now and then a great crash, as if a dish or kettle had been broken to pieces.

"Please, then," said Alice, "how am I to get in?"

"There might be some sense in your knocking," the Footman went on, without attending to her, "if we had the door between us. For instance, if you were *inside*, you might knock, and I could let you out, you know." He was looking up into the sky all the time he was speaking, and this Alice thought decidedly uncivil. "But perhaps he can't help it," she said to herself; "his eyes are so *very* nearly at the top of his head. But at any rate he might answer questions.—How am I to get in?" she repeated, aloud.

"I shall sit here," the Footman remarked, "till tomorrow—"

At this moment the door of the house opened, and a large plate came skimming out, straight at the Footman's head: it just grazed his nose, and broke to pieces against one of the trees be-hind him.

"—or next day, maybe," the Footman continued in the same tone, exactly as if nothing had happened.

"How am I to get in?" asked Alice again, in a louder tone.

"*Are* you to get in at all?" said the Footman. "That's the first question, you know."

It was, no doubt: only Alice did not like to be told so. "It's really dreadful," she muttered to herself, "the way all the creatures argue. It's enough to drive one crazy!"

Genuine argument is a disagreement which is justified with logical fact or a causal explanation, using such words as "because." Let's look again at the argument between Alice and the Footman. This argument is classified as primitive and not genuine because there is no attempt to make sense; the Footman makes disconnected statements which do not really answer Alice's questions or prove his point.

As children grow and relinquish their egocentric speech forms, true conversation begins to develop. This shift from egocentric to socialized speech indicates that children are able to understand more abstract thoughts and concepts.

CHAPTER 6

Discovering Space, Time, and Numbers

"Is this the place where numbers are made?" asked Milo as the car lurched again, and this time the Dodecahedron sailed off down the mountainside . . . until he landed sad side up at what looked like the entrance to a cave.

"They're not made," he replied, as if nothing had happened. "You have to dig for them. Don't you know anything at all about numbers?"

"Well, I don't think they're very important," snapped Milo, too embarrassed to admit the truth.

"NOT IMPORTANT!" roared the Dodecahedron, turning red with fury. "Could you have tea for two without the two—or three blind mice without the three? Would there be four corners of the earth if there weren't a four? And how would you sail the seven seas without a seven?

"If you had high hopes, how would you know how high they were? And did you know that narrow escapes come in all different widths? Would you travel the whole wide world without ever knowing how wide it was? And how could you do anything at long last," he concluded, . . . "without knowing how long the last was? Why, numbers are the most beautiful and valuable things in the world."

—*The Phantom Tollbooth*

E ven though a child may be able to count by rote or recite multiplication tables, he may not understand what these numbers signify. Milo certainly hasn't grasped the essential meaning of numbers or what they are used for—perhaps, that's why he doesn't like arithmetic. Piaget recognized the important distinction between using numbers and understanding what they are used for, between counting by rote and understanding that each number stands for one unit. He began research into how children develop concepts of number in the 1940s and, with his collaborators Bärbel Inhelder and Alina Szeminska, expanded his investigation into many different areas: sets, part-whole relationships, time, space, geometry, movement, speed.

There is a visible period of transition as the child moves from preoperational to operational thought. Children at the preoperational stage (ages two through seven) tend to focus on a single attribute or perception of a situation and disregard all others. This has been defined previously as *centering*. For example, when identifying geometrical shapes, young children often confuse triangles, rectangles, and squares because they are attending to only one feature of the shape: whether it has angles or not. When very young children attempt to reproduce triangles, they draw a circle. One explanation for this may be the child's lack of motor coordination, but it is not only that; the child may not recognize the angularity of the shape. This is also true when children copy a square. As they begin to be aware of the feature of "angles," they recognize that an angle exists, and may attach the angle to the outside of the circle.

On the facing page are some examples of the way children copy squares. An operational child (ages seven through twelve) examines the shapes not only for presence of angles, but also for number of sides, length of sides, and symmetry of sides. He can integrate this information to identify the shape. But in between these two stages, there is the transitional period of intuitive thought, where the child, still swayed by perception, bases his judgments on intuitive reasoning. This transition from perceptions to intuition to operations will become clearer as we discuss specific mathematical concepts.

Conservation

Probably the most important development during the concrete operational stage is the understanding of conservation, which must pre-

Angles rounded or acute

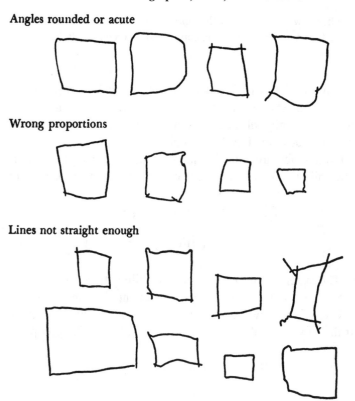

Wrong proportions

Lines not straight enough

cede the understanding of any other properties of number. Piaget used the term "conservation" to define the fundamental principle that objects or quantities remain the same despite a change in their physical appearance. In *Charlie and the Chocolate Factory*, Mr. Willy Wonka, the famed candy-maker, is trying to send a bar of chocolate by television from his factory right into children's living rooms. To do this, he insists, you need to send a *mattress-sized* bar of chocolate.

"It has to be big," Mr. Wonka explained, "because whenever you send something by television, it always comes out much smaller than it was when it went in. Even with *ordinary* television, when you photograph a big man, he never comes out on your screen any taller than a pencil, does he?"

Although an adult, Mr. Wonka is thinking much as a preoperational child does. The experiments on conservation are some of the most interesting, original, and thought-provoking of Piaget's studies, and will be described in some detail.

Children first acquire conservation of number. In a typical experiment, the child is shown two identical rows of buttons or pennies or

candies. The experimenter makes sure the child believes that the two rows are identical; the child may even count the buttons if she wishes. One of the rows is then spread out and the child is asked again if the rows have the same number of buttons. The preopera-

tional child invariably points to the longer row. The buttons are then pushed back into their original state, so that the child once again agrees that they are identical. Then one row is pushed closer together or arranged in a heap.

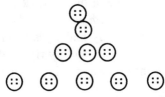

Each time a transformation is made the child is allowed to count the buttons if she wishes. Yet even with counting, the preoperational child insists that the denser row or heap contains more buttons. The experimenter can continue to collapse the row and spread it apart for half an hour and the child will not change her mind. It's so obvious to us that the number of buttons hasn't changed—why doesn't the child understand?

As in the other conservation experiments, a child at the preoperational level bases his answers on perceptual appearances. And once again, he is centering on the most compelling feature of the array— in this case, either the length or density of the row, but not both. He doesn't see that the buttons have undergone a perceptual (visual) transformation and not a change of quantity. When the child learns to conserve, he will understand that although the two rows don't look the same, they still contain the same number of buttons.

Let's go back now to the experiment on conservation of quantity that was described briefly in Chapter 2. In this experiment the child is shown two identical glasses of water or juice. The contents of one glass are then poured into a taller, thinner glass and the child is asked which glass contains more. The preoperational child is chained to visual appearances; the water level in the taller glass is higher, therefore that glass contains more water. Logical? Not really, but we must remember that the preoperational child's thought is not reversible. Even though she has actually seen, and can imagine, the action of water being poured from the short glass to the tall, thin glass, she is unable to imagine the reverse process (pouring the water back into the original glass). If the child could reverse the action in her mind, she would realize that the amount of water hadn't really changed.

Piaget performed other similar experiments. Children were asked, for example, to match one glass for every bottle in a row, or put one flower in each vase, or place one egg in each eggcup. Once again, the preoperational children matched objects according to the length of row, ignoring the number of objects in the row or the distance between objects. For example, the child would place a bottle in front of the glass at each end of the row, and then proceed to fill in the row with twice as many bottles as glasses. Some children put several flowers in each vase. At this stage, they had no conception of what a one-to-one correspondence was.

In a related experiment, Piaget handed children eight candies for the first day, with the instructions that four were to be eaten in the

Classification

morning and the other four to be saved for teatime. He then gave them eight more candies for the next day, but this time seven candies were to be eaten in the morning and one at tea. Piaget questioned the children to see if they understood that the number of candies to be eaten on both days was equal. As expected, the preoperational children didn't see that they had the same number of candies for each day because they hadn't yet acquired the notions of one-to-one correspondence or conservation of number. The day they had seven candies in the morning there was more candy for the day because it *looked* like more. The concrete operational children, however, understood that eight candies can be divided in more than one way.

This concept of *equivalence of sets* is illustrated by the following passage from *The Phantom Tollbooth*. On their journey to Digitopolis, Milo, Tock, and the Humbug reach a sign which says

DIGITOPOLIS	
5	miles
1600	rods
8800	yards
26,400	feet
316,800	inches
633,600	half-inches
AND THEN SOME	

"Let's travel by miles," advised the Humbug, "it's shorter."
"Let's travel by half-inches," suggested Milo, "it's quicker."

Both Milo and the Humbug, thinking as preschoolers would, base their decisions on a single perception—the Humbug on the number of units (regardless of the distance covered by each unit) and Milo on the size of each unit (regardless of how many of those units have to be traveled). If they were able to coordinate the two factors (as any operational child could) they would instantly realize the equivalence of the sets: 5 miles is equal to 633,600 half-inches.

Preoperational children also have difficulty in ordering objects in a series. When asked to line up sticks of unequal lengths according to size, the preschooler is bound to mix up the order. He goes through much trial and error before he succeeds, picking up each stick and comparing the sticks one by one. A child in the concrete operational stage understands *seriation*. He looks at the group of sticks, perceives their size relationships and instantly arranges them in order. He understands the concept of ordinal numbers (1st, 2nd, 3rd, et cetera) as well as that of cardinal numbers (1, 2, 3, et cetera).

Classification

One of the major concepts acquired during the concrete operational stage is *classification* of objects. Preoperational children may classify by a system which makes sense to them, but they don't always stick to the rules they choose. Classification is made upon perceptual characteristics. At one point, Piaget's children defined "daddies" as anyone who smoked a pipe, for Piaget was seldom seen without his meerschaum. At a later time Piaget wrote:

> we passed a man. Jacqueline inquired, *"Is that man a daddy?"*— What is a daddy?—*It's a man. He has lots of Luciennes and lots of Jacquelines.*—"What are Luciennes?"—*They are little girls and Jacquelines are big girls.*

Jacqueline was three years old at the time of that conversation and very egocentric. Since *her* father had daughters named Lucienne and Jacqueline, then that became the defining characteristic for the class of all daddies.

Preschoolers also experience problems with classes when faced with part-whole, some-all relationships; Piaget called this the *inclusion of classes*. This involves the idea that an object can be part of several classes at the same time, with some classes being part of larger classes. Piaget named this operation *nesting*. Rebecca Gibbs, age eleven, in Thornton Wilder's *Our Town*, understands this concept as she tells her brother George about a letter her friend received:

REBECCA: . . . He wrote Jane a letter and on the envelope the address was like this. It said: Jane Crofut; the Crofut Farm; Grover's Corners; New Hampshire; the United States of America.

GEORGE: What's so funny about that?

REBECCA: But listen, it's not finished: the United States of America; Continent of North America; Western Hemisphere; the Earth; the Solar System; the Universe; the Mind of God—that's what it said on the envelope.

GEORGE: What do you know!

REBECCA: And the postman brought it just the same!

Piaget conducted a very interesting experiment on part-whole relationships. He presented children with a box containing twenty wooden beads, most of the beads painted brown and only two beads painted white. When Piaget asked the children if there were more wooden beads or brown beads, the three- to five-year-olds would always answer that there were more brown ones. They seemed to understand that *all* the beads were wooden, and that *some* were brown and others white, but they still insisted that there were more brown beads. They *saw* more brown ones, and didn't consider the fact that a bead could be brown and wooden at the same time. They could not think simultaneously of the whole and its parts, that the class "wooden beads" contained both subclasses "white beads" and "brown beads." The six-year-old child in the following passage is just beginning to understand part-whole relationships.

BIS (6;8): Are there more wooden beads or more brown beads?— *More brown ones, because there are two white ones.*—Are the white ones made of wood?—*Yes.*—And the brown ones?—*Yes.*—Then are there more brown ones or wooden ones?—*More brown ones.*—What color would a necklace made of the wooden beads be?—*Brown and white* (thus showing that Bis clearly understood the problem).—And what color would a necklace made with the brown beads be?— *Brown.*—Then which would be longer, the one made with the wooden beads, or the one made with the brown beads?—*The one with the brown beads.* . . . Thus, in spite of having clearly understood, Bis was unable to solve it by including the class of brown beads in the class of wooden beads!

As the child moves into the stage of concrete operations she will be able to coordinate the two characteristics "color" and "wooden," understanding that a brown bead is not only part of the class "brown beads" but also part of the larger class "wooden beads."

A related part-whole axiom is "If two equal parts are taken from two equal wholes, the remainders will also be equal." Piaget studied the development of this concept with his "Cows on the Farm" experiment. Children were shown two identical sheets of green cardboard, which represented fields or pastures, and the children established the fact that the pastures were the same size. A wooden cow was then placed in each field and the children were asked whether each cow had the same amount of grass to eat. All the subjects said yes. The experimenter then placed a model farmhouse on one of the fields and asked again if the cows had the same amount to eat. All the children responded that this was not the case, and that the pasture without the farmhouse had more grass available. Then an identical farmhouse was placed on the second field, and the question of "Do the cows have the same amount to eat?" was repeated. Once the child established the fact that once again the cows had the same amount, the experimenter placed another farmhouse on the first farm, then the second farm, then a third house, et cetera—each time repeating the question, "Do the cows have the same amount to eat?" The only difference between the two farms was that on one the experimenter scattered the houses all over the field, and on the other he placed them next to each other in a corner of the field. The responses

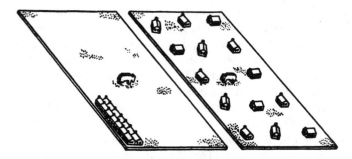

Figure adapted from Piaget, Inhelder, and Szeminska, *The Child's Conception of Geometry*, p. 262.

of the children were similar to those of the other conservation and part-whole experiments. The youngest children based their judgments entirely on perceptual appearance: The farm with the houses neatly arranged in a corner *looked* like it had more grazing area. Up until age five and a half or six, the subjects based their answers on intuition and perception. When the placement of the houses was identical (as in the very first transformation), they could see that the remainders of the wholes were equal. But when the array was different, the children became confused. At ages seven and a half to eight, the children could recognize that not only were the remainders of the whole equal, but that area was conserved.

As children move into the stage of concrete operations, and thought becomes reversible, children relinquish the tendency to reason solely on perception. They no longer regard numbers as names or objects, but symbols which represent amounts or quantities. This transition to operational thought is illustrated in *The Phantom Tollbooth* with a familiar arithmetic concept: averages. Milo meets half a child "who has been divided neatly from top to bottom." He tells Milo

"Oh, we're just the average family . . . mother, father, 2.58 children. . . . Every average family has 2.58 children, so I always have someone to play with. Besides, each family has an average of 1.3 automobiles, and since I'm the only one who can drive three-tenths of a car, I get to use it all the time."

"But averages aren't real," objected Milo, "they're just imaginary."

Spatial Relationships

From the studies on number and quantity, a logical move is to Piaget's work on the child's discovery of spatial relationships—or "spontaneous geometry," as he called it. This research is focused primarily on the development of intelligence as it works on spatial relationships, that is, application of Piaget's stage theory to the child's development of a notion of space.

Newborn infants have virtually no conception of spatial relations or constancy of shape. Through repeated interaction with the environment and handling of different objects, the child becomes familiar with shapes, assimilating them into his schemata.

There are three basic types of geometric concepts. Euclidean geometry, concerned with shapes and angles, is historically the earliest development. Projective geometry (problems of perspective) appeared later, and topology, which deals with concepts of proximity (nearness), separation, and enclosure, was the latest development. Yet in a simple experiment, Piaget came to the conclusion that children develop geometrical concepts in the reverse order of historical discovery! In this experiment, children aged three to seven manipulated objects behind a screen so that the objects were visible only to the experimenter. As Piaget anticipated, the youngest children could recognize by touch only familiar household shapes, such as scissors, combs, and keys. At age three and a half to four years, children could also recognize open and closed rings, curves, and flat surfaces with holes punched in them. These are known as topological forms. Only the older children could name the simple shapes: triangles, circles, and squares. Piaget found that once the topological concepts were mastered, notions of projective and Euclidean geometry could develop.

Piaget devised another ingenious experiment which illustrates this progression: he studied how children learn to tie knots. Piaget found that the very young children he observed had no idea of how a knot is made. They could not tie knots by themselves nor copy a model of a knot, even when being instructed how to do so. They did understand the difference between open and closed curves, but could not grasp the principle of intertwinement. All they made with the piece of string was curves and loops.

Children aged five and six years old could tie simple knots, because they understood the topological property of surrounding or enclosure. But they were unable to make a mental picture of the process of knot-tying. This became obvious when Piaget showed two identical knots, one loose and one tight. The child would deny that both knots were made the same way because they *looked* different. Thus, centering on one perceptual characteristic of the knot—tightness or looseness—influenced the child to ignore the process of *how* the knot was made.

Piaget also noticed that the five-year-old children could "recognize either tight or slack knots when they are compared with visually identical models, but won't say that they're the same as soon as the comparison knot is tighter or slacker than the model: in other words, as soon as one of them takes on a different appearance." By age seven, children have acquired reversibility of operations, and understand that knots are really continuous curves, which can be tightened, loosened, then tightened again.

The young child also has difficulty discriminating between two different perspectives of the same object. Piaget called this *spatial egocentrism*. An egocentric child of two, three, or four thinks that hers is the only viewpoint. She just doesn't understand that things might look different from someone else's point of view. She may see her bedroom as being neat and clean and can't understand why her mother has declared it a disaster area. In *Harold and the Purple Crayon*, Harold is trying to get back into his bedroom from his adventures outside. He draws a lot of windows with his crayon, trying to find his own, but can't seem to find the right one. Finally, Harold recognizes his bedroom window by the distinguishing feature of the moon being framed by it. He cannot imagine that it looks different to people walking down the street.

Piaget discovered quite by accident that this egocentrism is the primary characteristic of the young child's spatial perspective. While taking his son Laurent for an automobile ride in the country one day, Piaget observed that Laurent didn't recognize the Salève, the familiar mountain which rises behind the city of Geneva. Piaget knew that his son could point out the mountain from his garden window, yet from this new perspective, it wasn't the same mountain to Laurent at all!

Piaget devised an experiment to test the child's confusion over different perspectives. He set up a scale model of three mountains and had his subjects look at the mountains from all different perspectives by walking around the model. Each child was then seated in a chair on one side of the model, and a doll was placed in a chair directly opposite the child, on the other side of the model. Piaget then asked the child to choose from a set of drawings the one that represented the *doll's* view of the mountains. All the young children

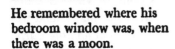

He remembered where his
bedroom window was, when
there was a moon.

It was always right around
the moon.

Spatial perspective and egocentrism

picked the same drawing—the one that was the view they saw from their chair! Piaget then asked the child to switch places with the doll, and once again to choose the doll's view. Again, the child chose the picture which showed what she was looking at. The child was unable to assimilate the view she had seen just a moment ago from the other seat into her schema. Piaget found that the ability to coordinate perspectives doesn't appear until the age of nine or ten, well into the stage of concrete operations.

Piaget's investigations into how children develop concepts of measurement provide insight into how they develop conceptions of space. In a famous experiment, Piaget and his associates showed children a model tower built on a low table. The tower was built of twelve blocks of assorted shapes and sizes. The children were asked to build a tower of the same height on another table—a table of a different height. Subjects were provided with assorted building blocks and wooden sticks of different lengths. The ways in which children of different ages attempted to reproduce the tower are intriguing. The youngest subjects, about four years of age, measured with the naked eye, estimating the heights of the two towers. In addition, they built their towers to be the same height as the model, ignoring the fact that the two tables were of different heights. Some children even used the wooden sticks provided to "measure" by laying a stick across the tops of the towers to see if it would balance.

Children who were one or two years older, but still in the preoperational stage, recognized the need for some sort of measuring standard. They used their bodies. Some children stood next to the model tower to see how high it came up to on their body (e.g., up to their nose) and built the tower accordingly. Other five- to seven-year-olds, aware of the difference in table heights, used a "fingertip to elbow" measure, or measured with their hands, running back and forth between towers keeping their hands apart as if they actually held the distance between them.

It was the seven- and eight-year-old children who came up with the idea of using the wooden sticks provided as rulers. At first, they would use the sticks in the same manner that the five-year-olds used their bodies—marking off a point on a very long stick which indicated the length of the whole tower. Finally, they realized that they could use shorter sticks and count multiples of the sticks to measure height. Because they understood the concept of "the whole is equal to the sum of its parts," the children were able to "divide" the tower into parts in order to measure it.

Time

When children go to visit relatives who live far away, they often confuse concepts of space and time. If a child's grandparents live three hundred miles away, and the child visits them by plane, the trip might take one hour. In the child's mind, he believes that his grandparents live closer than his uncle, who lives in a closer town which is three hours away by car. The hours required in transportation define the notion of distance for the child.

Piaget began studying children's conceptions of time at the urging of Albert Einstein, whom he met in 1931. Einstein was interested in how children learn the principles of time and speed, and the relationship between the two. Piaget found that children interpret time concepts in a completely different way from adults. Just as time and space were confused, time is often equated with and mistaken for "distance" or "speed."

Understanding time concepts is contingent upon an understanding of the concepts of velocity and uniform motion. Adults comprehend the equation Distance = Velocity × Time because they regard time as a constant. Yet the young child often confuses time with distance, while speed is overlooked. For example, in one experiment, children watched mechanical snails or cars race across a tabletop. The car which was "fastest" was always the one which stopped ahead of the others. Thus, time is conceived of as a place.

Time is thought of as a place in many other ways. Psychologist David Elkind believes that children think of bedtime or suppertime as places because "it is only suppertime when you are at the table and bedtime when you are in bed." Similarly, children take the dates on the calendar quite literally. As is evident from the cartoon on the opposite page, for Charlie Brown, spring begins when the calendar says so—regardless of the weather outside.

Applying the misconception of time-speed, children at ages five and six also believe that work completed first is the easiest and quickest. Again, time is thought of as a place or stopping point, with the duration of the work being neglected. When the child works quickly, time passes quickly; when he works slowly, time passes slowly. In the cartoon on page 91, Dizzy believes that quick-sand is so named because it moves quickly (this another example of the realism of words discussed in Chapter 3). As he sees it, the more quickly the sand flows, the faster the time will pass and the sooner his piano practicing will be over.

In relation to this notion, Piaget performed an experiment where children worked at some task, such as putting marbles in a jar, while sand fell through a sandglass. As anticipated, the younger subjects all asserted that the sand fell faster when they worked harder. They had not yet separated the concepts of time and action; nor did they understand that time is a continuous flow. It is not until the stage of concrete operations at age seven or eight that the child begins to understand the constant flow of time. Only with this understanding can the child learn to tell time with some understanding of what time means.

One of an elementary school child's biggest accomplishments is learning how to tell time. Even if a child knows how to read the hands of a clock, he may not understand the relationships of clock time, calendar time, and historical time.

Children often confuse the two concepts of succession (past, present, future; before and after) and duration (number of minutes, days, or years). The child grasps the present before he can understand the time sequence of events. The "future" is the last concept that he learns.

Let's examine the child's confusion of historical time and calendar time. At the preoperational level, the child's conception of time is, as expected, dominated by egocentrism. She may regard the past as whatever came before her, but has no conception of duration of the past, or of past events in relation to the present.

For preschool children, a "long time ago" refers to a day last week as well as events last summer. You may have overheard a child say to his mother, "Remember when I cut my finger a long time ago"; that event could have happened a day, a week, or a year ago. In the same way, the child has trouble understanding that if you

Realism

announce a visit to the zoo for the coming Sunday, he has to wait out the week. On Tuesday, he begins nagging and asking, "Is tomorrow Sunday?" In order to help the child gain a sense of the future and waiting period, parents or teachers might actually mark off each day on a calendar. Though a child has grasped the notion of succession, he has not yet coordinated it with the notion of duration of time.

This "time confusion" also appears in preschool children's notions about age and birth order. Their basic misconception is "the taller a person is, the older he is." Age is confused with height. Once a person has stopped growing, he's also stopped aging. However, all

Time confusion

adults are considered to be old. One little boy told Piaget that his grandfather was "old right away."

This can be attributed to the child's centering on a single perceptual cue (height) which we have seen many times before in the child's development of numbers concepts. And, of course, egocentrism dominates the reasoning of the preoperational child. She doesn't understand that an adult is older because he has lived for more years; that adult exists for the child only from the time he came into the child's life.

In the transition to the operational level of thought, the child begins to separate the factors of age and height. Alice in *Alice's Adventures in Wonderland* is making such a transition. Once inside the White Rabbit's house, she drinks an unlabeled bottle of liquid and grows until she fills the room, her head touching the ceiling and one arm hanging out a window.

> "There ought to be a book written about me, that there ought! And when I grow up I'll write one—but I'm grown up now," she added in a sorrowful tone, "at least there's no room to grow up any more *here.*"
>
> "But then," thought Alice, "shall I *never* get any older than I am now?"

Though Alice is still confusing age with height, she senses that her logic is faulty. She knows she isn't grown up yet, but since she's grown in size so much, she necessarily *must* be older.

Age and height confusion

Five- and six-year-old children, in the intuitive period of thought, know whether they are older or younger than a friend or sibling, but cannot tell you who was born first. Flexibility and reversibility of thought are not present at this age, and the child cannot coordinate the two factors, age and date of birth. In addition, a child must be able to use the concepts of one-to-one correspondence and seriation in order to understand that an increasing sequence in age corresponds with a decreasing series of dates of birth. It is not until the operational level that a child understands that if he is seven and his sister is four, then he is three years older, but his sister was born three years *after* him. These are difficult concepts to master. This is illustrated by Dour, a child in one of Piaget's experiments.

DOUR (7;5)
"How old are you?"
"7½."
"Have you any brothers or sisters?"
"No."
"Any friends?"
"Yes, Gerald."
"Is he older or younger than you?"
"Five years."
"Was he born before or after you?"
"I don't know."
"But think about it, haven't you just told me his age? Was he born before or after you?"
"I could ask him."
"But couldn't you tell without asking?"
"No."
"When Gerald will be a father, will he be older or younger than you?"
"Older."
"By how much?"
"By five years."
"Are you getting old as quickly as each other?"
"Yes."
"When you will be an old man what will he be?"
"A grandfather."
"Will he be the same age as you?"
"No. I'll be five years less."
"And when you will be very, very old, will there still be the same difference?"
"Yes, always."

It is not until the operational stage that children can coordinate succession and duration. In an experiment that studied this relationship, Piaget showed children pictures of two trees, one bigger than the other, and asked them which tree was older. Almost invariably, he found that the younger children believed the bigger tree to be older, simply "because it is bigger." But the older children, who were able to separate the concepts of age and size, replied that they could not answer the question without knowing when the two trees were planted.

According to Piaget, the child can only develop an abstract sense of time once he understands that time is a constant flow. Most children at the preoperational level do not grasp the notion of uniform flow of time, and therefore depend upon speed and distance in order to "measure" time. The preoperational child, in his egocentric manner, believes that he can stop time, speed it up, or slow it down.

CHAPTER 7

Learning About Right and Wrong

Parents may be baffled when their children lie, cheat, break the rules in a game, invent their own rules, or even deny that rules exist. Some parents wonder if their child is going to remain dishonest forever; others wonder in what way they have failed to inculcate in their child the moral codes of civilized society.

Piaget believed that morality develops through successive stages just as intelligence, play, and language develop systematically. Each successive stage leads to a higher level of moral awareness, and each stage corresponds to the cognitive growth of the child. Piaget delineated three stages of moral reasoning: (1) the premoral stage (until age four), where a child feels no obligation to rules; (2) the conventional or heteronomous stage (about four to seven years), where rules are obeyed literally, adults are seen as all-powerful, and one is obliged to submit to the power and punishment of older children and adults; and (3) the autonomous stage (about seven to twelve years), where the child reviews and considers the purposes and consequences of rules, and considers obligations to be based on reciprocity and exchange.

In *The Moral Judgment of the Child*, Piaget describes how children develop a sense of rules, notions of stealing, lying, clumsiness; and finally, how children develop a sense of justice and regard for punishment. By questioning the child and recording his answers, Piaget was able to follow a child's ideas of right and wrong.

The Stages of Rules

It was partly through the observation of children's games—marbles, in particular—that Piaget developed his understanding of the development of rules, and through his posing of simple stories with dilemmas that Piaget developed his theory of a child's morality. If you observe children below the age of seven at play, you can see them elaborate their own rules, adapt them to specific situations, change them at will, and yet believe quite seriously that they are playing *with rules*. Piaget delineated four successive stages that deal with the practice or application of rules which roughly follow his three main stages of morality. They are as follows:

1. Motor or individual character, 0–2 years
2. Egocentric, 2–7 years
3. Cooperation, 7–11 years
4. Codification of the rules, 11–12 years and on to adulthood

Motor or individual character stage. Before the age of two, the child plays in a more or less ritualized manner. If given a small ball, he enjoys it for its own sake—the color, texture, the rolling movement. He may roll a ball into a cup, drop one into a pail, or hide it under a pillow. The games are simple and rely on motor activity and the joy and delight of the reappearing ball. There are no rules. The pleasure and satisfaction do not come from winning but from the repetition of the act, and in a small way from the development of a skill. The youngster may even attempt to "eat" the ball and in his simple games nibble or taste it.

This primitive form of play is most vividly exemplified in *Winnie-the-Pooh*. Pooh and Piglet presented Eeyore, the donkey, with a pot and a balloon for his birthday. On their way to see Eeyore, Piglet falls, the balloon bursts, and becomes a "small piece of damp rag." Eeyore is at first dismayed about the fate of the balloon, but becomes excited when he sees the pot. He invents a simple game.

Eeyore picked the balloon up with his teeth and placed it carefully into the pot. . . . picked it out and put it on the ground, and then picked it up again and put it carefully back. Pooh and Piglet are elated that Eeyore has discovered a simple game.

> "I'm very glad," said Piglet happily, "that I thought of giving you Something to put in a Useful Pot."
> But Eeyore wasn't listening. He was taking the balloon out, putting it back again, as happy as could be. . . .

Egocentric stage. This stage between the ages of two and seven is a transition between purely individualized behavior and the socialized play that follows. The child's pleasure in this stage is derived from participating in a group or, as Piaget described, in the "honorable fraternity" of those who know the game. Preschoolers enjoy playing in the presence of others (parallel play), even though they may not always watch or interact with them. They feel a communion with the abstract, ideal adult who epitomizes fairness and justice, but at the same time they may be inventing their own rules throughout the game. Children in this stage copy and try to imitate the play of older playmates, and their play parallels the egocentric stage of language development. Their conversations rarely have true socialized interactions involving opinions, commands, ideas, information. Their speech is pseudo-conversation or the "collective monologue" discussed in Chapter 5. Although the child begins to be aware of rules, her rules are indefinite and highly individualized. As the child grows older she begins to respond more to other children and more interaction takes place. However, there is no real interest in competition or winning. Sometimes the child elaborates on her own rules and even changes them, or the play sequence itself, to accommodate her own needs. A child may tell another child what to do and her only justification will be, "Because *I* say so."

In *Alice's Adventures in Wonderland*, the Dodo invents a Caucus Race for the prime purpose of drying all the creatures who had become wet from Alice's "pool of tears." In response to Alice's query about the race, the Dodo replied, "The best way to explain it is to do it." The racecourse was marked out in a circle, with everyone placed along the course "here and there." There were no rules. "There was no 'One, two, three and away!' but they began running when they liked, and left off when they liked, so that it was not easy to know when the race was over." When the race was indeed "over," the Dodo decided that everybody had won and "all must have prizes."

This example demonstrates the child's lack of structure about the game, his failure to have rules, and the arbitrariness of the rules. Further on in the story, Carroll again presents us with another example of egocentric morality. The croquet game of the Queen employed live hedgehogs for balls, flamingoes for mallets, and soldiers doubled over for arches.

> The players played all at once, without waiting for turns, quarreling all the while, and fighting for the hedgehogs; and in a very short time the Queen was in a furious passion, and went stamping about, and shouting, "Off with his head!"

Cooperation stage. The child at about age seven begins to develop a sense of cooperation. Winning becomes important to children now, but along with this emerges a sense of mutual control, unification of rules, and agreement within a game. However, even within this stage, Piaget found that although a child may play with rules while engaged with the group, his private interpretation of the rules is individualistic. For example, Piaget described the play of two boys, Mac and Wid, who often played marbles together. When Piaget played with each one alone he noted: "Not only do they tell us of totally different rules . . . but when they play together they do not watch each other and do not unify their respective rules even for the duration of one game." Not until the last stage will children be able to completely internalize rules and understand that rules are consistent and unchanging. Alice, who is approaching this stage in her moral development, is aware of the faulty reasoning of all the creatures in Wonderland. Her comments concerning the Queen's croquet game reflect her maturing sense of morality.

> "I don't think they play at all fairly," Alice began, in a rather complaining tone, "and they all quarrel so dreadfully one can't hear oneself speak—and they don't seem to have any rules in particular: at

least, if there are, nobody attends to them—and you've no idea how confusing it is all the things being alive!"

Codification of the rules stage. The fourth stage, reached between eleven and twelve years of age, involves the strict, fixed codification of rules. The rules are understood by all players and observed by society as a whole. Thus, when young boys in this stage play marbles they view a rule as something "built up progressively and autonomously." The rules will eliminate the need to quarrel. They can be changed and modified by the group, and they are no longer an external, coercive "revealed truth." Children at about age eleven begin to feel more on the level of adolescents and adults and begin to free themselves from adult constraint. There is an increasing respect for rules and the belief that one can introduce modification of rules by "legal channels." In *Lord of the Flies*, a band of boys marooned on an island must develop a set of rules in order to survive. They are still too young to maintain the law and order, and their "society" breaks down resulting in cruel acts toward each other and death for Piggy, the intellectual child. Piggy actually asks the important question that is a theme of the book, "Which is better—to have rules and agree, or to hunt and kill?"

Certainly, Alice cannot understand the court of justice that is assembled by the King and Queen of Hearts. Laws are arbitrary in Wonderland, changed completely at the whim of the Queen, and trials are a mockery. For example, the judge is the King, the jurors confusedly write nonsense on their slates, sentences are handed down at whim before verdicts are given. Quarreling and lack of order and discipline are typical of the court procedure. Alice, although only seven and a half, is aware of the ridiculousness of the trial and feels somewhat proud that she can recognize the "muddle" of the court. Her own growing sense of justice enables her to discriminate now between arbitrary rule-making and a universal code.

Moral Realism

In addition to "rules of the game" children in the preschool stages deal with morality in a more egocentric manner than school-age children. Younger children tend to ignore the intention of an act and deal with the result of the action. For example, in a situation involving stealing or lying, the child who "steals the most" or tells the "greatest lie" is considered *more* guilty than a child who steals *one* object or tells a little lie. The preschool child calls a liar "naughty," but the liar who "saw a dog as big as a cow" is the "naughtiest" according to Piaget's subjects. Indeed, the children also believe the naughtiest child deserves the most punishment. The preschool child regards any act that shows an obedience to a rule or to an adult a "good" act, and any that does not conform a "bad" act. In addition, this belief, or as Piaget called it, *moral realism*, demands obedience to the letter rather than the spirit of the law. Finally, because the child takes rules literally, she evaluates acts not in accordance with the "motive that has prompted them, but in terms of their exact conformity with established rules." As the child matures, she leaves the stage of moral realism and adult constraint, and begins to obey the rule itself, not just the command of the adult. The child of seven, for example, begins to recognize that a lie is bad in itself—punished or not.

The preschool child also accepts the notion of *immanent justice*—that objects have within them the power to punish. For example, if a child plays with matches and is burned, he reasons that the "burn" was his punishment because he disobeyed. In *Winnie-the-Pooh*, Pooh falls into a gorse bush while trying to steal some honey, and as he puts it:

> "It all comes, I suppose," he decided, as he said good-bye to the last branch, spun 'round through time, and flew gracefully into a gorse-bush, "it all comes of *liking* honey so much. Oh, help!"

Object Responsibility

Clumsiness. Piaget dealt with the child's notion of responsibility for his acts. The preschool child generally judges an act by its consequences rather than by its intention. For example, if a child is called to dinner, opens a door, and by mistake knocks down a tray containing fifteen cups, and they all break, she would be judged *more* guilty than a child who broke *one* cup while "stealing" a cookie. Clumsiness, Piaget felt, is a normal part of the preschool child's life and leads to continuous conflict with adults. The cartoon on the opposite page illustrates this point.

Lying. Very young children in the *premoral stage* may lie without feeling any guilt. Parents are constantly explaining to these children what is fact and what is fiction. Sometimes a lie makes a child feel important, and sometimes the child's vivid fantasy life makes a made-up story seem very real to him. Children in the *conventional stage*, below the age of seven, describe a lie as "saying naughty things." For example, when Piaget questioned a child, Tul, aged six, Tul insisted "fool" is a lie "because it is a naughty word." He may know that "lie" means not telling the truth, but nonetheless equates lies with "naughty words." As Piaget wrote about the preschool child:

> When he pronounces certain sentences that do not conform with the truth (and which his parents regard as genuine lies) he is astonished to find that they provoke the indignation of those around him and that he is reproached with them as a fault. When he brings in certain expressive words from the street the same thing happens. He concludes that there are things one may say and things one may not say, and he calls the latter "lies" whether they are indecent words or statements that do not conform with fact.

By the time children reach the age of seven, they can distinguish between a lie and a naughty word. For example, older children recognize that a lie is antisocial and is contrary to the notion of mutual respect and reciprocity. Alice, "a very truthful child," must try to defend herself against the unjust accusations of the Pigeon, who insists she is a serpent.

> "Well! What are you?" said the Pigeon. "I can see you're trying to invent something!"
> "I—I'm a little girl," said Alice, rather doubtfully as she remembered the number of changes she had gone through that day.
> "A likely story indeed!" said the Pigeon, in a tone of the deepest contempt. "I've seen a good many little girls in my time, but never one with such a neck as that! No, no! You're a serpent, and there's no use denying it. I suppose you'll be telling me next that you never tasted an egg!"

Clumsiness

Alice cannot lie and admits that she has tasted eggs. The Pigeon still does not believe Alice, but Alice is willing to take her chances and receive the Pigeon's wrath.

During the elementary school years, the child still has an external conscience. He still believes that rules are operating outside of him and the adults are benevolent, well-intentioned, and powerful. A child in this stage also enjoys outwitting the clever adult, as Huck Finn's escapades illustrate. When Huck sneaks out at night and tries to fool the Widow Douglas and her sister Miss Watson, who "pecked" at him all the time to study and learn his prayers, or when he tries to fool Mrs. Loftus by disguising himself as a girl, he knows he's lying and violating the moral code of these elderly ladies, but really does not care. He just does not want to be "sivilized." Although the child between seven and twelve can differentiate between the lie and the truth as Alice could, he still sees rules as laid down by adults, and obeys them for fear of punishment. The child of seven through twelve loves fantasy, mystery, magic, the supernatural, and adventures dealing with outer space, distant places, and distant times. The enthusiasm among preadolescents for movies such as *Jurassic Park* and *E.T.* and television's *Ghostwriters* and *Star Trek* attests to the lure of such fare. The appeal of the adventure story lies in the uncertainty and doubt, and the eventual control and mastery in the resolution. The seven- to twelve-year-old comes to grips with his own doubts, and reaffirms the notion of justice and truth as the characters resolve their conflicts. Thus the child gains a sense of mastery as he watches the story develop and conclude.

Peter Pan has great appeal for children because Peter never grows up, yet Peter has a "code" that he and his boys follow. In *The Adventures of Huckleberry Finn*, we see Huck's dilemma concerning his own conscience and the code of the adults around him. Huck has moved out of the conventional stage of morality and is moving into the autonomous stage. He may at times cleverly deceive adults and follow his own "savage" code, but his own developing sense of morality prevents him from betraying the runaway slave Jim to his would-be captors. Huck cannot accept the prejudices of the adult community and tells a lie. He must then grapple with his conscience:

"They went off, and I got aboard the raft, feeling bad and low because I knowed very well I had done wrong, and I see it warn't no use for me to learn to do right; a body that don't get *started* right when he's little, ain't got no show—when the pinch comes there ain't nothing to back him up and keep him to his work, so he gets beat. Then I thought a minute, and says to myself, hold on,—s'pose you'd adone right and give Jim up; would you felt better than what you do now? No, says I, what's the use you learning to do right when it's troublesome to do right and ain't no trouble to do wrong, and the wages is just the same? I was stuck. I couldn't answer that."

Huck expresses quite clearly the dilemma of many young teenagers—how to accept an adult code when their own sense of fairness is at odds with it.

Problems of Punishment and Justice

"That's three faults, Kitty, you've not been punished for any of them yet. You know I'm saving up all your punishments for Wednesday week—Suppose they had saved up all *my* punishments?" she went on, talking more to herself than the kitten. "What *would* they do at the end of a year? I should be sent to prison I suppose, when the day came. Or—let me see—suppose each punishment was to be going without a dinner: then, when the miserable day came, I should have to go without fifty dinners at once! Well, I shouldn't mind *that* much! I'd far rather go without them than eat them!"

As Alice scolds her kitten in *Through the Looking Glass* she is using what Piaget calls *expiatory punishment*. This is punishment of an arbitrary character, that is, there is no relation between the content of the guilty act and the type of punishment that is meted out. Some further examples of expiatory punishment for a young child would be forcing him to write his name fifty times, taking away his favorite toy, or hitting him. In *Alice's Adventures in Wonderland*, the Mad Hatter and March Hare try to stuff Dormouse into a teapot, simply because he has difficulty trying to relate a story. The young child may issue this kind of expiatory punishment to his toy, or as in Alice's case to her kitten, and by doing so may be copying the kind of punishment that an adult has arbitrarily inflicted on him. Indeed, the Red Queen used expiatory punishment as her only method of coping with transgressors: "Off with his head!"

Preschool children generally suggest using expiatory punishment for offenders. As they reach school age they move in the direction of reciprocity punishments—to paraphrase Gilbert and Sullivan, the punishment should somehow fit the crime. Reciprocity also includes the idea that a wrongdoer must "long for a return to normal relations" as a consequence of his just and fitting punishment. Piaget delineated six forms of reciprocity punishment: exclusion, when the child is excluded from a game because he "cheats"; material consequences, when the child gets no milk for dinner because she refused to buy some when there wasn't enough in the house; depriving the transgressor of the thing he has misused—if a child tears a page in a book he may not be allowed to read the book; reciprocity proper— the child breaks the toy of a child who has broken hers; restitutive punishment—one puts to right the material damage, i.e., a child fixes the window he broke, or he pays for it; and censure—no punishment takes place, but the child is made to feel that she has transgressed by appealing to her sense of guilt—her conscience.

In *Winnie-the-Pooh* and *Alice's Adventures in Wonderland* we find numerous examples of both expiatory and reciprocity punishment. For instance, Rabbit and Piglet decide to play a trick on Kanga, and substitute Piglet for Baby Roo, resulting in Piglet hopping into Kanga's pocket. Rabbit scampers off with Roo, and Kanga hops to her home. When she discovers Piglet in her pouch instead of Roo, she decides to punish Piglet by pretending she thought he was Roo, and then proceeds to give Piglet a bath. This form of reciprocity punishment, material consequences, follows naturally out of Piglet's deception:

> Before he knew where he was, Piglet was in the bath and Kanga was scrubbing him firmly with a bathing flannel.
> "Ow!" cried Piglet. "Let me out! I'm Piglet!"
> "Don't open the mouth, dear, or the soap goes in," said Kanga. "There! What did I tell you?"

Kanga was doing exactly what adults do when the bond of mutual trust is broken—deliberately simulating credulity. Kanga plays along with Piglet's original intent to deceive her, and as a result Piglet, who hates baths, is given the punishment as a consequence of his deception. The use of censure is found among older children, and not until age eleven or twelve do children really understand the concept of personal responsibility. In *The Little Prince* the King puts it very well when he decides to make the Prince his Minister of Justice. When the Prince reminds the King that there are no people on the King's planet and there would be "nobody here to judge," the King wisely says:

"Then you shall judge yourself. That is the most difficult thing of all. It is much more difficult to judge oneself than to judge others. If you succeed in judging yourself rightly, then you are indeed a man of true wisdom."

And indeed, when children reach this stage, when they have internalized a sense of justice through "progress made by cooperation and mutual respect—cooperation between children to begin with, and then between child and adult as the child approaches adolescence and comes, secretly at least, to consider himself as the adult's equal," then one can say the child has truly developed a code of morality.

CHAPTER 8

Beyond Piaget: Using His Theory for Teaching, Learning, and Parenting

Although Piaget did not attempt to solve education problems through classroom intervention, his prolific writings on the science of education have influenced educators everywhere. Piaget was critical of the educational practices during his lifetime. He stated in *Science of Education and the Psychology of the Child* that there were three central problems in education: He was concerned about what the aims were in teaching children, what subjects were to be taught, and what methods were to be used. Piaget listed obstacles in education that created the above problems. First, he claimed that "pedagogy is a science" and one that has not been helped by other sciences. Second, he saw the teacher as "constrained" to follow set programs and methods dictated by state authorities while other scientists such as physicians had closer links to university faculties or professional organizations. Piaget also complained about the lack of "scientific dynamism" in the applied science of teaching when compared with the "pure" sciences. Finally, he commented on the poor training of teachers at both primary and secondary levels. He saw a need for more linkage between the universities and the schools, and a need for more research emphasis in the teacher-training curriculum.

Piaget was particularly adamant concerning the education of preschoolers. He insisted that the preschool child be given every opportunity for the development of sensory-motor functions "in the full sense of free manipulation." His recommendations to the International Conference on Public Education as early as 1939 contained provisions for sensory-motor education, and the request that reading, writing, and arithmetic be left for the primary grades. Piaget emphasized that preschool teachers need specialized theoretical and practical courses of instruction in order to help the children learn through sensory-motor manipulations. If the teacher is well trained, she can help the child through sensory-motor education discover "numerical notions and forms." The child will get preparation through these "first steps in numerical and spatial intuition" for the logical operations and subsequent language that develop.

Most educators recognize that the preschool years are critical in the development of a child's intellectual, social, and emotional growth. Programs such as Head Start stress the importance of early learning. Psychologists agree that children learn important things in the first three years of life. Can a theory such as Piaget's be applied in a systematic way so that parents and teachers can help children attain the skills or operations of each of Piaget's four stages of development?

One of Piaget's last books, *The Grasp of Consciousness*, dealt with the child's understanding of how certain tasks—walking on all fours, building a ramp for toy cars, pulling a small rectangular box by a string along a plank of wood—are performed. The numerous experiments in the book involve tasks of practical intelligence. Through interviews with children, Piaget attempted to discover how the children thought each task was performed. He found that although the children could do the tasks, they generally were inaccurate in their explanations as to the reasons for their successful completion. The children ranged in age from four through adolescence, and at each stage of development, Piaget found a different explanation for these physical acts. He suggested that there are degrees of consciousness, each depending on different degrees of integration. A child will gradually move to the highest level of consciousness by the time he is eleven or twelve and will be capable of theorizing and varying factors in an experiment. The child must be given opportunities for active exploration of materials in order to understand how certain phenomena take place. It is only through such manipulation of objects that the child can begin to understand the operations of his acts.

Much of Piaget's theory can be used in teaching and learning. This chapter will focus on specific ways in which a parent or teacher can use Piagetian concepts in helping a child grow.

A child learns through two methods: physical knowledge and logical knowledge. If a child plays with materials such as pegs, clay, beads, or blocks, she is using her senses to learn about physical properties such as shape, size, length, and height. As she builds her castle out of blocks, she learns that large blocks support smaller ones in order to make a turret. She learns that clay can be flattened to look like a cookie or rolled to resemble a sausage. She learns that it feels sticky and can be rolled smooth. She learns that there are different colors of beads. Through active participation and sensory exploration, she gains physical knowledge about her materials.

Children also gain logical knowledge: the development of concepts such as relationships of objects through size, shape, and color; the development of numbers and quantity such as less, more, equal; and notions about space and time. As the child plays with blocks, he learns that blocks can be plastic, wood, or cardboard. He is developing a schema or mental picture of blocks as things that have particular qualities. He also learns that he can arrange these blocks according to shape, line them up from small to big, learn that he has a few or a great many blocks. He may also learn that three small blocks equal one large block as he builds his castle turret, and thus he begins to explore the concept of measurement.

As children play, they learn that they can sort across classifications by putting all red blocks together even if they are of different sizes or shapes, or put all round blocks together even if they are red, blue or yellow. Playing, also, with toy cars of different sizes and colors and sorting them by size first and then by color can help a child learn to classify and then sort across classifications. Toys and materials, however, must match the child's developmental level. If a child is moving from one stage to another, e.g., a transition between preoperational and concrete operations, he may benefit from play with materials that encourage his exploration of the more advanced concepts of the latter stage. Piaget stressed that a child only learns when he is biologically able to form a new schema. A child who is not ready to match yellow cars with yellow cars may play with cars using them only to move along the ground, and he may group them in a haphazard fashion. A child who is ready to classify will group by color, size, or by kind of vehicle.

Nursery schools and day-care centers are beginning to look at "play" in a more serious manner, and teachers are recognizing that a child can learn through play. Play can contribute to learning, and as discussed in Chapter 4, has considerable benefits for the social, emotional and intellectual growth of the child. The nursery school teacher or child care worker who is familiar with Piaget's theory can supply materials and create an atmosphere conducive to the active exploration that is part of a three- or four-year-old's normal routine.

Nursery schools in America have continuously developed curricula reflecting each new trend in education. In the 1960s, the Montessori movement proved to be a challenge to the traditional middle-class child-oriented schools of that period. Maria Montessori developed her curriculum to meet the needs of slum children in Italy. Her program was practical, including self-help skills such as tying laces, buttoning clothes, washing hands and faces. Her aim was to teach children to become independent. In addition, the schools emphasized structured activities, exercises for muscle development and games that involved all the senses. Children learned how to sort materials, how to match colors, shapes, sizes, and how to recognize numbers and letters. They were taught how to talk with soft voices, and how to move their bodies to varying rhythms. The most important contribution, however, was the notion of motivation. Maria Montessori believed that if the materials were available and interesting, a child would be motivated to explore them fully. Children would repeat acts in order to gain mastery over them and be competent. She felt, as did Kurt Lewin and, later, Robert White, two distinguished psychologists, that the intrinsic reward was the mastery of an object and the feeling of competence that results. When a child learns she can pour water into glasses from a pitcher, or that she can put pegs into varying size holes, or that she can recognize shapes such as circles, squares, and rectangles, she feels good about herself as an effective, competent individual.

The Montessori movement was not widespread, despite its advantages for children who needed such opportunities to develop intellectual and social skills. The influence of the British infant schools for children aged five to seven in this country in the late 1960s and 1970s was even more powerful than the Montessori philosophy. The infant schools are public, government-supported schools utilizing an individual learning approach. Although classes are large, thirty-five to forty children in one room, children work in small groups. There is more emphasis on the value of play in the British infant curriculum, but the thrust is still cognitive with a learning-by-doing approach. The British system recognizes that a child can learn through play, and that the teachers can guide a child to develop concepts and language skills through his natural desire to play. The teachers are trained to introduce learning elements into play. For example, if a child is pouring tea for her doll, the teacher can use this to introduce the concept of conservation. A child can begin to learn that a specific amount of tea in a large cup would be equal in amount to tea in a small cup.

Currently, nursery schools and day-care centers are trying to combine the best elements of both movements—the structured-learning approach, and the informal, learning-through-play approach. In many nursery schools, a part of the day is allotted to free play while another part is geared to more directed activities such as beginning reading and number recognition. Educators recognize the notion of "observational learning" or the informal learning that takes place through active participation in real situations where the meaning of a word or idea is intrinsic to the contents. A child learns about hammers, for example, when he helps an adult pound a nail into a piece of wood. He learns that the nail joins two pieces of wood together by performing the task himself. Learning by doing in some experimental schools helps many children deal with some of the physical and social situations that they will meet outside of school.

Adapting Piaget's Ideas
for the Classroom or Home

Let us examine some of Piaget's ideas and see how they can be adapted into a nursery school curriculum. Four main areas of intellectual development seem to fit neatly into the nursery school or day-care center activities—classification; number, space, and time; seriation or ordering; and finally, language development. The following are some ideas that parents and teachers could use and embellish upon. Most of these ideas do not require fancy toys or expensive educational aids, but rely on materials found in the home.

Classification. Children can be given the opportunity to sort buttons, plastic lid covers, spools of thread, bottle caps, pieces of wool. They can sort according to color, size, or shape. The first step is to just sort by one concept, or *simple* sorting. After children have learned to sort by a single property, they can learn that objects may have two common properties such as color and shape. They may then sort out the objects that are both red and round, or blue and square, and perform what Piaget called *multiplicative classification.* The next step is for children to learn that in a grouping of yellow triangles and yellow squares, *all* the shapes are yellow, but some are triangles and some are squares.

Finally, children, through their manipulation of their toys, can learn that there are subclasses of objects. They can learn that yellow beads and red beads are part of the larger class of wooden beads or *class-inclusion* relations. The actual playing with materials and the exploration of their properties through feeling, looking, touching enables a child to learn these concepts even before he can explain their relationships in verbal terms.

Number, Space, and Time. Children begin to count in a rote fashion. *Sesame Street* has helped many children learn to count from one to ten, but the physical correspondence of objects on a one-to-one basis can only be learned by actual manipulation of the objects that are to be counted. For example, a child may count out five buttons. If she does not actually touch each button as she says the number, she may find herself skipping one and counting to *four*, although *five* are on the table. First, the child learns to count by looking at and touching the objects. Counting on fingers is the way most children begin. The nursery rhymes of "This Little Piggy" or "Ten Little Indians" help the child see the items to be counted. Later she can visualize the number and begin to understand that numbers are symbols.

When a child has practiced counting and seems to understand a one-to-one relationship, you might try teaching conservation. Training preschoolers to conserve is a controversial issue among educators. Jerome Bruner, a prominent psychologist, questions Piaget's assumption that children are not ready to conserve until age seven. Evidence gathered by Bruner and Gruen suggests that one can teach the concept of conservation before a child has reached this age. Work by Almy shows that children who conserved early were more advanced on certain psychological tests: reading readiness and logical thinking, for example. Mermelstein and his co-workers were unsuccessful, however, in attempting to train children of kindergarten age to conserve substance. Most researchers feel that language interferes with the child's grasp of conservation principles. Words such as "more," "less," "equal," "same," "different" may be unclear to a child although he actually perceives differences. The practice of counting objects can nevertheless do no harm, even if the child fails to grasp the notion of conservation at such a young age.

Children at about the ages of six and seven can be taught that the ten objects divided into sets of five and five are numerically equivalent to ten objects divided into sets of two and eight or one and nine. They can be taught that the whole, in this case the number ten, is conserved even when the additive composition of its parts is varied. This step in a child's intellectual development is necessary before he can comprehend simple arithmetic problems.

Using small blocks and placing them in assorted groupings after the child has counted them will help him understand this operation. For example, if you use ten blocks, let the child count them first. Ask him to divide the blocks into any smaller grouping he may wish. Then have him count the blocks in each group and then count all the blocks he has. He will begin to see that ten remains ten no matter how he groups the blocks. In just this way you can demonstrate conservation by using two sets of ten buttons—one set to remain in a fixed position, and one set to be transformed by spreading them out or by piling them into heaps. The child will soon see that the number ten is a constant and that the appearance of the set does not alter the quantity.

Games dealing with conservation of area, using cars or trucks lined up on a square piece of paper, can demonstrate to a child that there is the same amount of parking space whether cars are placed in even rows or scattered on the square. You can use miniature farm animals, all of the same size, and scatter them on a square piece of green paper, or line them up in one corner of the square. A child can see that there is just as much grass for the cows or lambs to eat no matter where the animals are placed. Measure the square so that the child understands that the area remains the same and that only her perception of the grass is altered by your placement of the figures. Teaching children about space concepts such as "in front of," "in back of," "under," "over," "inside of," "outside of" can be done by using a miniature figure and a little house made of blocks. Simple instructions such as "place the doll or soldier in front of the house" or "in back of the house" will motivate a child to learn these concepts because he will perceive this as a game. The game can become more complex if you use two figures and add some suspense. For example, the game might involve a "dragon" who is hiding "in back of" the house. You might ask the child to find the "dragon." Taking turns by allowing the child to issue the commands gives him practice and helps him to incorporate the concepts into his vocabulary.

Many children below age five confuse left and right. If a child sets the table and places a fork to the left side of a plate, he cannot set the place opposite his in the correct fashion unless he physically moves around to that place. By practice, such as moving a placemat completely around so that a child *sees* where the fork goes when he moves to the opposite place, a child gradually understands that the left-right positions will be reversed. Piaget calls this inability to see things from any but one's own point of view *spatial egocentrism*. Playing house, or car wash, or fort, and using toys to shift positions help the child deal with concepts such as up, down, left, right, above, under, near, far, in, out.

Puzzles readily available in toy stores can be used to help a child learn part-whole relationships. Snap-type blocks or Tinker Toy blocks enable children to put objects together, take them apart, and learn about three-dimensional relationships.

One of the most difficult concepts a child has to understand concerns the notion of planes. When children below age seven draw a house, they tend to place the chimney perpendicular to the sloping sides. They seem not to know that the horizontal and vertical axes are constant. If you build a clay mountain for a child, and use some miniature figures to climb this mountain, the child begins to see that the figure's feet remain horizontal to the table or floor. The child by age seven grasps the notion that the table or floor should be used as reference points in making judgments.

Children also learn about space by playing rhythm games. For example, as a child imitates her parent's or teacher's movements, she can raise a left hand, right hand, touch her nose, touch her toes, stretch her arms out in front, overhead—simple exercises to help her understand geometric planes. She can learn about speed by running to fast music, or moving as slowly as she can to music with a slow beat. She can learn about balance by hopping on one foot, or walking along a balance beam, or by trying to stand still on one foot.

Time sequences can also be learned through play and exercises. A child who plays "school" or "party" learns that there are preparations made before the game begins, that there are time sequences for each part of the game, and that he will put things away after the game is over. If he bakes cookies, he learns to wait for them to bake and sets a timer to signal completion; if he plants a seed, he can actually mark off each day on a calendar as he watches it grow and blossom. A child can make his own "clock" out of a paper plate. A brass fastener in the center holding a paper hour and minute hand allows the hands to be turned. Using different colors, write each number on the plate. The child can "set" his clock for various activity times during the day—9:00 for breakfast, 10:00 for a story, 12:00 for lunch, et cetera. Marking off days on a calendar as a special holiday is approaching gives the child a sense of time, as well as an opportunity to rehearse numbers in sequence. Watching the movements of the sun in the sky helps an older child to approximate the time of day. Doing a chore together and estimating how long you and a child think it will take before you begin, and then checking the actual time it took, also gives the child a sense of time duration. Walking to a friend's house or running there can be timed and compared and made into a game: How slowly can I walk? How quickly can I run? How long did it take for each? Write the times down and let the child keep a little record book.

Seriation or Ordering. Children confuse notions about size and age. When they reach seven, they begin to understand that taller people are not necessarily older people. A preschooler has difficulty lining up dolls, sticks, or blocks of varying heights. Allowing the child to practice looking at these differences gives the child opportunities to form an image about size variation. A parent or teacher could use materials found in the house to practice ordering. Items such as pipecleaners cut into different lengths, candles of different sizes, plastic container lids, even silverware can be used to help the child learn about ordering.

Playing games such as "find me the smallest, find me the tallest," could be used to make the task more challenging to the preschooler. A child who lines up cars and trucks by size is practicing ordering. The child who plays "parade" with her dolls is practicing ordering. Through play, children can begin to see size differences and learn at their own pace.

We have included some references at the end of this chapter that can help a parent or teacher plan some exercises based on Piagetian principles. We feel that the child must actually be ready for such instruction, and imposing a "lesson" on a child who is unwilling or too young may be frustrating for both parent and child. A parent or teacher should respect the child's desire to learn. Materials should be available, but not forced on a child. Just a few minutes of play with purpose each day is sufficient. Parents must remember that there are individual differences among children in their attainment of concepts and language skills.

Language. Language development, especially, occurs among children at different rates. Girls tend to speak earlier than boys, but by school age, both sexes have equal vocabulary. There are some exercises described below that parents and teachers can use with their children to foster language development. Many preschool programs have a "language arts" program in their curriculum. Piaget believed that as the structures of thought become more refined, more language is necessary for the achievement of this elaboration. However, Piaget offered little instruction concerning how to attain language skills.

Many psychologists and educators have designed programs to encourage language development by emphasizing such concepts as roundness, squareness, and class inclusion. Basically, a language arts program consists of art, drama, discussions, and opportunities for manipulation of materials. Materials readily available in a well-furnished nursery school can stimulate speech. Children can talk about their paintings, their carpentry efforts, the seeds they plant, their rock collections, the "cake" they baked out of mud or sand. Children also need to have their ideas written down in a scrapbook, on a "word wall" (a huge piece of oaktag), on a blackboard, in a simple newspaper, in a word file, or in a picture-and-word file. They also need practice in talking. "Show and Tell," tape-recording their stories, acting in a puppet show, making up a song, compositions, or their own "book" to share are all useful activities. Stimulating materials such as books, computers, records, tapes, supplies for dramatization, and musical instruments will help language to develop.

Most of all, children need parents to listen to them and to talk with them. The young mother who babbles, sings, or talks to her baby is paving the way for language. Educators believe that parents are the prime source of language development if they get in the habit of sharing and discussing ideas with their children. The evening meal can be a good time for parents to listen to their children and to encourage language. A story at bedtime offers a child new vocabulary and concepts. Explanations about new items or sights you see when you shop or travel or when the class goes on a field trip, help the child build vocabulary. Research by Singer, Caldeira, and Singer indicates that children who score higher on tests of imagination and are rated as highly imaginative in free play also have a better grasp of language. Encouraging children to express their ideas in play and in conversation helps them to develop language skills. Children want to talk about things that happen to them. As you may recall from the chapter on language, they engage in monologues, or collective monologues, and talk even when no one is listening. Using their natural inclination to talk and helping them find the correct word or expression can be done in an atmosphere of play. Talking on a toy telephone to a child and playing puppet show are ways in which you can encourage language expressiveness without making language a lesson. Chanting, reciting nursery rhymes, and playing finger games are delightful ways in which language can be used.

Research has demonstrated that role-taking is useful in helping a child grasp verbal instructions and then apply them accurately. A child could be asked to place a picture on the table in a position which would permit the teacher or parent to view the depicted figure right side up or upside down. The child of course would see the picture upside down if he oriented the picture so that the teacher could see it. The adult and child could take turns making the verbal request and performing the act. Such performance tasks enable children to better understand the difficult verbal concepts relating to perspective.

Prekindergarten Screening

There have been many tests developed by psychologists and educators to determine which skills children have before they enter kindergarten. Many school systems carry out prekindergarten or kindergarten screening programs to assess a child's cognitive and social skills in order to help make better class placements and plan for individualized programs of study. Currently there are hundreds of prekindergarten screening tests available ranging from local school assessment procedures that have only local normative data to those published by the larger test companies, and that have been validated on hundreds of preschoolers. The question remains: Are we searching for an I.Q. measure or for a list of skills that a child can perform that matches the normal developmental age of the child? Also, should we test such young children in the first place?

It is true that children change so rapidly in the preschool years that any instrument that purports to measure a particular cognitive function is subject to error. The one advantage of prekindergarten screening, however, is that gross deviations from the norm can be detected such as language deficits, perceptual difficulties, and even physical disorders such as vision and hearing losses. For these reasons alone, any sound prekindergarten testing is valuable. Remediation programs in early years of schooling can prevent serious learning and social adjustment problems that might emerge if such difficulties were neglected.

Although there are many preschool tests available, such as the Bayley Scales of Infant Development and The McCarthy Scale, there are fewer tests that are based primarily on a Piagetian framework. Most of the tests yield I.Q. scores or scores that are similar to general intelligence scores.

One test based on Piagetian concepts is the Program Evaluation Measure (PEM) used in Baltimore by the Early Admissions Program. The test assesses the child as he enters the preoperational period at about age two and through age seven. The test, administered at monthly intervals rather than at one period of time, evaluates the following: (1) ability to identify, name and describe concrete objects including people, animals, toys; (2) ability to express ideas in conversation; (3) ability to solve a problem; (4) ability to classify by form, size, color, and function; (5) ability to develop skills in auditory perception; discriminate, memorize, recall, and reproduce; (6) ability to demonstrate motor perceptual skills and identify, name, and describe body parts and functions; orient one's body to different kinds of space, coordinate eye-hand and eye-foot actions; (7) ability to identify, match, compare sets of objects, count, understand addition and subtraction; (8) ability to develop wholesome feelings about himself through his performance on tasks; and (9) ability to use art as a form of self-expression.

We have described these criteria because they evaluate the child in a variety of ways, and measure his rate of development over a long period of time. A teacher or parent can focus on an area of weakness and help the child improve. These nine areas follow Piaget's developmental patterns which we discussed in this book. Children attain the above skills at varying rates. With this test, no child is penalized by an I.Q. number, but is evaluated qualitatively, and in a way that identifies weaknesses and strengths.

Because of dissatisfaction with I.Q. measures, schools are now often using the kind of assessment described above. The main advantages of this kind of approach are that the measures are based on a theory of cognitive growth rather than a notion of I.Q. such as the Wechsler scales or Stanford-Binet intelligence test. The tests like the Baltimore model rely less on verbal facility; and the items themselves can be used to teach in an individualized program.

Psychologists familiar with Piaget's theory could devise their own informal measures to assess preschoolers—and design a program that fits the unique abilities of each child. Test items developed by a teacher or psychologist could be based on a variety of Piaget's concepts such as animism and causality (what does *living* mean, why do objects float); time, movement, and speed; classification, numbers, space, conservation tasks (such as number, liquid, volume, area); and language (ability to adapt information, question, criticize, comment).

A Word About Television and Piaget

The influence of television

In an earlier book, *The House of Make-Believe*, one of the authors has described how parents can use television more effectively with their preschoolers. A child should not be a passive viewer. There actually can be cognitive and social gains if parents would interact with their children as they view programs together. Research has shown that children who watch programs such as *Barney & Friends*, *Mister Rogers' Neighborhood*, and *Sesame Street* make social and cognitive gains if there is adult intervention as they view.

Currently there are parent guides available to be used in conjunction with these three programs, and local public television stations can supply information concerning how to obtain them. These materials are part of a national outreach program of the Public Broadcasting Service to help parents use television as an educational tool. The activities presented in the guides are related to particular concepts on the television programs. For example, *Mister Rogers' Neighborhood* deals with concepts of past and present by using a theme of remembering. Activities include finding photos of a child or parent when each was younger, remembering a special trip and then drawing a feature of that trip, or finding a toy that was special when a child was younger and then talking about it. Activities that relate to a particular *Barney & Friends* program about colors include the use of sponge painting to draw particular colors on brown paper bags, which then could be used as gift bags. *Sesame Street* guides include activities related to learning about Puerto Rico, for example, through the use of songs, dances, maps, and globes.

We realize that parents cannot always watch television with their children, but even a few minutes in front of the screen can be productive if the parent carries out one or two simple activities after the program ends. The following suggestions are meant to stimulate parents and teachers and lead to a creative use of television.

When you watch television with a child you can direct the child to educational programs such as public television now produces: *Barney & Friends, Shining Time Station, Sesame Street*, or good commercial programs such as *Ready, Set, Learn*, or a locally produced education program listed in your newspaper. Find the character your child most enjoys from one of these programs, and use it (in the form of a puppet you make, or a cardboard version you draw of it) to be the main character in simple make-believe games. Here are some ideas based on Piagetian principles—just a few samples to start you off.

The alphabet game (for letters and words). Have your child identify characters or objects on his favorite television show that begin with a particular letter. For example, if he likes *Barney & Friends*, ask him to name a character from that show that begins with the letter B (Baby Bop) or D (Derek).

The size game (for concepts—big-small-more-less). Find something *small* on the program; find something *big* on the program. Find something *small* in the kitchen; find something *big* in the kitchen. Ask who had *more* things to do or say on the show.

Things that go together (for classification). Where are all the square things on the program? Find things that are round; find colors that match; find animals. Match by functions—things that ride; things to eat; things to drink; things to wear.

Weather (causality). Watch the news together. Talk about the weather. Keep a chart to see if the weatherperson is correct. Make a paper sun, paper clouds; draw raindrops, snowballs. Pin the correct drawing on your chart each day. Here causality can be made into a game leading to understanding of scientific facts.

Music (concepts of slow, fast). When music plays, have your child move to the beat. Let her know which is fast or slow. Clap hands in rhythm to help get the beat.

Riddles (for language development). Play a game with your child where you become a TV character. Ask the child to "guess who I am." Describe the character and see if your child can guess who it is. Let him have a turn being a character. This can help build expressive language skills.

Picture book (recognition and language development). From your newspaper or magazine, cut out pictures of television characters and paste them on construction paper. Ask your child to tell you about the person, and put all the characters who belong together in a pile.

When a program is over, select an incident that was related to socializing behavior. (*Mister Rogers' Neighborhood* is particularly good for constructive social behavior.) Rehearse one social theme with your child. For example, if Ernie on *Sesame Street* or King Friday on *Mister Rogers' Neighborhood* shared an object that day, play sharing with your child. Play sharing with dolls or puppets first; later your child may share his crayons and cookies with his brother or sister. Taking turns can be practiced in just this way. Discussions about jealousy, fear, love, anger can be stimulated by the television format.

VCRs, Computers, and CD-ROMs

Current technology has opened the way to many new ways of imparting information to young children. The amount of time spent watching television has increased over the years for families from about 4.5 hours per day in 1950 to 7.5 hours each day in the 1990s. Currently, 98 percent of American households have a TV and approximately two-thirds of American households own a VCR. Despite the proliferation of computers, video games, CD-ROMs, laser discs, and the future integration of such technology to allow for more interactive possibilities, television still remains the main delivery system of entertainment to young children.

Ernest Boyer, president of the Carnegie Foundation for the Advancement of Teaching, stated in his book, *Ready to Learn: A Mandate for the Nation*, that "next to parents, television is the child's most influential teacher" (page 140). He recommended that the major networks should offer at appropriate times at least one hour of preschool educational programming every week. Our suggestions on the following pages mesh with Boyer's recommendation—that materials should be made available for parents and educators to use in conjunction with specific children's programs.

We believe that parents can also use VCRs, CD-ROMs, or computer games with children to enrich their experiences. There are catalogs available that list the latest software for children, and reviews of new products can be found in such publications as *Parent's Choice* or in the media sections of local newspapers. Videos can usually be borrowed from local libraries. An advantage of a video is that a parent can control the choice of content, prescreen the video, and of course play it again if a child truly enjoys the program.

CD-ROMs require special equipment, but if a parent has a computer and does invest in a CD-ROM attachment, even three-year-olds can quickly learn to move a "mouse" and in effect cause particular icons to appear on the screen at will. The CD-ROM allows for some interaction rather than the passivity of merely watching a television program. Computer games serve this same interactive function. There are several companies that have geared math, science, and nature concepts to young children's intellectual abilities, and these products appear to stimulate learning.

An excellent book by Merle Marsh demystifies the commercial on-line services such as America Online, CompuServe, eWorld, GEnie, and Prodigy and offers general information about on-line bulletin boards, internet resources, and terminology. Marsh also offers parents numerous suggestions to help their children learn how to use these computer services. Included are activities designed for preschoolers, children ages six to eight, nine to twelve, and thirteen to eighteen and beyond.

Suggestions for Parents

Finally, here are some suggestions that might help parents in using television more effectively:

- Screen programs before your preschooler starts viewing television.
- Allot a specific time of day for TV viewing and limit this time.
- A V chip embedded in television sets can block out programs parents deem are unsuitable. There are also control boxes available that enable parents to use a timing device to block out specific programs as well as entire channels.
- Encourage children to talk about programs they watch, and discuss them with your children.
- Watch programs with your child for a few minutes each day. Use the materials later in ways we have suggested.
- Discuss the commercials. Help children understand that there may be exaggerations about a product.
- Help children delineate between reality and fantasy so that when

they watch a program they will not imitate fantastic behavior such as the stunts on *Lois and Clark* and *Batman*.

- Use television as an active learning tool. Wherever possible look for ideas that you can model from the program. If Mister Rogers plants seeds, why not you, too? The active participation in even a small project like this helps the children learn some simple science facts.
- Be candid about your dislikes in a show. Encourage children to become discriminating viewers.
- If your ethics or morals are in contradiction to those shown on a show, discuss this openly with your child.
- Encourage even a preschooler to "write" a letter in favor of or in opposition to a show. Help him express his feelings. Let him know early that the consumer of television can be heard via his comments to the producers. Fred Rogers and Barney the Dinosaur receive many letters from preschoolers.
- Provide toys, games, books, and other materials that offer alternatives to TV viewing. Actively use these materials with your child.
- Finally, engage your child in play, try to take her on visits to local sites, museums, the library, the firehouse, the zoo—all the places that stimulate and encourage your growing child.

Jean Piaget has given us much to think about in raising our children. He believed that the practical intelligence of a child, its "spontaneous grasp of the physical world will enable it to succeed in predicting phenomena long before it can explain them." Practical adaptation in infants is the "first stage of knowledge." Providing children with an environment conducive to exploration, and offering our children time to share their ideas with us is perhaps the most important ingredient in developing their intelligence.

Glossary

Accommodation: See *Adaptation.*

Adaptation: Involves the processes of *assimilation* and *accommodation*. It is the way in which an individual adjusts to his environment. First he gathers ideas, information, perceptions, experiences into existing mental models. This first step is *assimilation*. Accommodation is the modification of new information and actions to form a new mental plan or schema.

Animism: The belief that everything in nature has consciousness and life.

Artificialism: The belief that natural events such as mountains, lakes, rivers, sun, rain are made by man.

Assimilation: See *Adaptation.*

Centration: The focusing or centering on one aspect of an object and disregarding its other features. It is difficult for a child to explore all aspects of a particular stimulus. By the age of six or seven a child can decenter, or focus on all aspects of a stimulus and incorporate them into a total plan or pattern.

Circular reaction: The repetitive actions of a baby in order to maintain a change in the environment that had occurred by accident. A baby who kicks a rattle hanging over his crib sees it move. He tries to make the rattle move again by reaching for it with his foot.

Classification: The grouping of objects by similar properties.

Cognition: Mental activities such as thinking, reasoning, remembering, perceiving. The process by which the seemingly random information presented by the environmental and social stimuli around a person is organized into meaningful units for memory and ultimate action.

Collective monologue: Conversations of preschool children who talk to each other but not in a way that is related to what each child is saying. The conversation is egocentric. Each child deals with his own ideas and interests.

Compensatory play: A child expresses his emotions and conflicts through play. When a child is jealous of a new sibling, his game may consist of sending "the baby" off on a long trip.

Concrete operations: The child thinks in terms of concrete, existing objects. He is able to conserve, order, classify, but does not hypothesize or use abstractions. It is the third stage of intellectual development in which the child is not yet ready to address "possibilities," but attends only to the given objects and figures in its environment.

Conservation: The ability to see that the qualities or inherent properties of objects do not change despite a change in physical appearances. Four ounces of water in a short, wide glass reaching the halfway mark are the same as four ounces of water in a tall, thin glass, where it rises to the brim.

Echolalia: Speech that repeats sounds and words. A child may echo his own speech or that of another person.

Egocentrism: The interpretation of all events in terms of one's own subjective experience. A lack of awareness that there are points of view different from one's own. The child who persists in egocentric thinking may believe that when his soup is hot, everyone's soup is hot.

Equilibration: The balance between the processes of assimilation and accommodation.

Euclidean geometry: Geometry concerned with shapes, angles, surfaces, volumes. Originated at the time of the early Egyptians.

Formal operations: This refers to the period from about age twelve through adulthood. The individual uses logic, forms hypotheses, and is able to evaluate moral situations in an autonomous way.

Genetic epistemology: A field which combines the study of biological contributions to intelligence with the theoretical study of knowledge.

Immanent justice: The child's belief that objects have within them the power to punish.

Juxtaposition: Thinking which links successive unrelated ideas, judgments, perceptions; they are collected but not related to each other in a meaningful way.

Ludic symbolism: In make-believe play a child uses an object to represent one that is not present—a broom becomes a horse, a walnut shell becomes a cup.

Maturation: The physical growth process through differentiation of the nervous system; mental structures develop, enabling the child to become capable of understanding his environment.

Moral realism: The belief that the punishment must be related to the act committed regardless of intent. A child who breaks more cups accidentally should be punished more severely than a child who breaks only one deliberately.

Object permanency: An object exists even when it is not directly visible or otherwise subject to the sensory experience of a child. A certain level of development is necessary before a child functions as if a hidden or forgotten object still exists in its own right.

Operations: An interiorized action—one performed in the mind. Operations permit the child to think about actions which he previously had to perform physically.

Parallel play: Children play alongside each other. They do not necessarily interact as they play. Each child is engaged in his own game and is not sharing or cooperative in a game.

Perception: Becoming aware of stimuli through the senses.

Preoperational: The second stage of development in which the child is dominated by egocentric thought and prelogical thinking. Perceptions rather than logic influence a child's judgment.

Realism: The child believes that what seems real to him must have an objective reality and must be real to others. When a child hears about the "population explosion," he expects to hear a boom.

Reciprocity punishment: The misdeed and punishment are related in content and nature. Piaget delineated six forms. Exclusion, material consequences, depriving the transgressor of the thing he misused, reciprocity proper, restitutive punishment, and censure.

Reversibility: The individual is able to mentally reverse the direction of his thought. By such a process we can add and subtract, or retrace our steps along a path.

Schema (pl. schemata): The mental framework which a person uses to interpret things he sees or hears. A schema organizes perceptions or behaviors and enables a person to understand his environment. Information we have gathered is stored in the form of organizational structures rather than in isolated bits and pieces. The term is used broadly by Piaget to signify both ideas and motor patterns of behavior.

Sensory motor: The infant relies on information about the world through his senses and motor activity. This is the predominant mode of the first two years of life.

Social transmission: The influential interactions with other people that enable a child to learn and adapt to his environment. Parents, teachers, and peers are all social influences on the child.

Symbolic play: The child uses something other than the original object to symbolize the object. Piaget's daughter plays with a walnut, pretending it's a pussy-cat. Symbolic play depends on assimilation without accommodation.

Syncretism: Thinking which involves combining unrelated ideas into a whole. A child attempts to relate everything to everything else.

Transduction: The child uses prelogical, egocentric thinking. He attempts to relate ideas that may not necessarily be connected. Inferences are made without logical reasoning. If a child skipped his nap, then there was no afternoon. If smoke came out of a train funnel, then it made the engine go.

References

CHAPTER 1

Works of Piaget

Piaget, Jean. "Autobiography." In E. G. Boring et al., eds. *History of Psychology in Autobiography*, vol. IV. Worcester, Mass.: Clark University Press, 1952, pp. 237–56.

———. *The Child's Conception of the World.* New Jersey: Littlefield, Adams & Co., 1965.

———. *The Origins of Intelligence in Children.* New York: W. W. Norton & Co., 1963.

———. "Piaget's Theory." In Paul Mussen, ed., *Carmichael's Manual of Child Psychology*, vol. I, 3rd ed. New York: John Wiley and Sons, 1970, pp. 703–32.

Piaget, Jean, and Bärbel Inhelder. *The Psychology of the Child.* New York: Basic Books, 1969.

Related Readings

Beilin, H., and P. B. Pufall, eds. *Piaget's Theory: Prospects and Possibilities.* Hillsdale, N.J.: Lawrence Earlbaum Associates, 1990.

Bullock, M., and R. Gelman. "Preschool Children's Assumptions About Cause and Effect: Temporal Ordering." *Child Development* 50 (1979): 89–96.

Elkind, David. "Jean Piaget—Giant in the Nursery." *New York Times*

Magazine, May 26, 1968; pp. 25ff. Also reprinted in David Elkind, *Children and Adolescents: Interpretive Essays on Jean Piaget*, 2nd ed., pp. 11–29. New York: Oxford University Press, 1974.

Flavell, John. *The Developmental Psychology of Jean Piaget*. Princeton, N.J.: D. Van Nostrand Co., 1963.

Gardner, H. *Frames of Mind: The Theory of Multiple Intelligences*. New York: Basic Books, 1983.

Ginsburg, Herbert, and Sylvia Opper. *Piaget's Theory of Intellectual Development*. Englewood Cliffs, N.J.: Prentice-Hall, Inc., 1969.

Isaacs, S. *Intellectual Growth in Young Children*. New York: Schocken, 1966.

Maier, Henri. *Three Theories of Child Development*, rev. ed. New York: Harper & Row, 1969.

Mandler, J. "A New Perspective on Cognitive Development in Infancy." *American Scientist*: 78 (1990); 236–43.

Meltzoff, A., and M. K. Moore. "Newborn Infants Imitate Adult Facial Gestures." *Child Development* 54 (1983): 702–709.

Sternberg, R. *The Triarchic Mind*. New York: Viking-Penguin, 1988.

Literature

Delessert, Etienne. *How The Mouse Was Hit on the Head by a Stone & So Discovered the World*. Garden City, N.Y.: Doubleday, 1971.

De St. Exupéry, Antoine. *The Little Prince*. New York: Harcourt Brace, 1943.

CHAPTER 2

Works of Piaget

Piaget, Jean. *The Child's Conception of Number*. New York: W. W. Norton & Co., 1965.

———. *The Construction of Reality in the Child*. New York: Basic Books, 1954.

———. *The Language and Thought of the Child*. Cleveland: World Publishing Company, 1955.

———. *The Origins of Intelligence in Children.* New York: W. W. Norton & Co., 1963.

———. *Play, Dreams and Imitation in Childhood.* New York: W. W. Norton & Co., 1962.

Piaget, Jean, and Bärbel Inhelder. *The Psychology of the Child.* New York: Basic Books, 1969.

Related Readings

Beilin, H. "Dispensable and Core Elements in Piaget's Research Program." *The Genetic Epistomologist* 13 (1985): 1–16.

Case, R. "Neo-Piagetian Theories of Intellectual Development." In H. Beilin and P. B. Pufall, eds., *Piaget's Theory: Prospects and Possibilities.* Hillsdale, N.J.: Lawrence Earlbaum Associates, 1992, pp. 61–104.

Flavell, John. *The Developmental Psychology of Jean Piaget.* Princeton, N.J.: D. Van Nostrand Co., 1963.

Furth, H. "A Contemporary Thinker from Psychology's Past." *Contemporary Psychology* 29: 25–27.

Gelman, R., and E. Spelke. "The Development of Thoughts about Animate and Inanimate Objects: Implications for Research." In J. H. Flavell and L. Ross, eds., *Social Cognitive Development: Frontiers and Possible Futures.* Cambridge: Cambridge University Press, 1981.

Ginsburg, Herbert, and Sylvia Opper. *Piaget's Theory of Intellectual Development.* Englewood Cliffs, N.J.: Prentice-Hall, Inc., 1969.

Maier, Henri. *Three Theories of Child Development*, rev. ed. New York: Harper & Row, 1969.

Singer, Dorothy G. "Pooh, Piglet and Piaget." *Psychology Today* 6, no. 1 (June 1972): 72ff.

Literature

Baum, L. Frank. *The Wizard of Oz.* New York: Random House, 1950.

De St. Exupéry, Antoine. *The Little Prince.* New York: Harcourt Brace, 1943.

Juster, Norton. *The Phantom Tollbooth.* New York: Random House, 1961.

Milne, A. A. *Winnie-the-Pooh.* New York: E. P. Dutton, 1926.

CHAPTER 3

Works of Piaget

Piaget, Jean. *The Child's Conception of the World.* New Jersey: Littlefield, Adams & Co., 1965.

————. *The Origins of Intelligence in Children.* New York: W. W. Norton & Co., 1963.

————. *Play, Dreams and Imitation in Childhood.* New York: W. W. Norton & Co., 1962.

Literature

Bagnold, Enid. *The Door of Life.* New York: William Morris & Co., 1938. Passage reprinted in Elliot Landau et al., eds., *Child Development Through Literature.* Englewood Cliffs, N.J.: Prentice-Hall, Inc., 1972, pp. 6–7.

Baum, L. Frank. *The Wizard of Oz.* New York: Random House, 1950.

Dahl, Roald. *Charlie and the Chocolate Factory.* New York: Alfred A. Knopf, 1964.

De St. Exupéry, Antoine. *The Little Prince.* New York: Harcourt Brace, 1943.

Eliot, George, *Silas Marner.* New York: Harper & Brothers.

Juster, Norton. *The Phantom Tollbooth.* New York: Random House, 1961.

Milne, A. A. *The House at Pooh Corner.* New York: E. P. Dutton, 1961.

————. *Winnie-the-Pooh.* New York: E. P. Dutton, 1926.

CHAPTER 4

Works of Piaget

Piaget, Jean. *Play, Dreams and Imitation in Childhood.* New York: W. W. Norton & Co., 1962.

Related Readings

Singer, Dorothy G., and Jerome L. Singer. *Partners in Play.* New York: Harper & Row, 1977.

――――. *The House of Make-Believe: Play and the Developing Imagination.* Cambridge, Mass.: Harvard University Press, 1990.

Singer, Jerome L., ed. *The Child's World of Make-Believe.* New York: Academic Press, 1973.

Literature

Brodkey, Harold. "Trio for Three Gentle Voices." from *First Love and Other Sorrows.* New York: Dial Press, 1958. Also reprinted in Elliot Landau et al., eds., *Child Development Through Literature.* Englewood Cliffs, N.J.: Prentice-Hall, Inc., 1972, pp. 12–17.

Carroll, Lewis. *Alice's Adventures in Wonderland.* New York: New American Library, 1960.

Hughes, Richard. *A High Wind in Jamaica.* New York: Harper & Row, 1928.

Milne, A. A. *The House at Pooh Corner.* New York: E. P. Dutton, 1961.

White, E. B. *Charlotte's Web.* New York: Harper & Row, 1952.

CHAPTER 5

Works of Piaget

Piaget, Jean. *The Language and Thought of the Child.* Cleveland: World Publishing Company, 1955.

Literature

Carroll, Lewis. *Alice's Adventures in Wonderland* and *Through the Looking Glass.* New York: New American Library, 1960.

De St. Exupéry, Antoine. *The Little Prince.* New York: Harcourt Brace, 1943.

Milne, A. A., *Winnie-the-Pooh.* New York: E. P. Dutton, 1926.

CHAPTER 6

Works of Piaget

Piaget, Jean. *The Child's Conception of Movement and Speed.* New York: Basic Books, 1970.

———. *The Child's Conception of Number.* W. W. Norton & Co., 1965.

———. *The Child's Conception of Time.* New York: Basic Books, 1970.

———. "How Children Form Mathematical Concepts," *Scientific American* 189 (1953): 74–79. Also reprinted in R. C. Anderson and D. P. Ausubel, eds., *Readings in the Psychology of Cognition.* New York: Holt, Rinehart & Winston, 1965, pp. 406–414.

———. *Play, Dreams and Imitation in Childhood.* New York: W. W. Norton & Co., 1962.

Piaget, Jean, and Bärbel Inhelder. *The Child's Conception of Space.* New York: W. W. Norton & Co., 1967.

Piaget, Jean, Bärbel Inhelder, and Alina Szeminska. *The Child's Conception of Geometry.* New York: Basic Books, 1960.

Related Readings

Elkind, David. "Of Time and the Child." In David Elkind, ed., *Children and Adolescents: Interpretive Essays on Jean Piaget,* 2nd ed. New York: Oxford University Press, 1974.

Flavell, John H. *The Developmental Psychology of Jean Piaget.* Princeton, N.J.: D. Van Nostrand Co., 1963.

Gelman, R., E. Meck, and S. Merkin. "Young Children's Mathematical Competence." *Cognitive Development* 1 (1986): 1–29.

Terman, Louis, and Maud Merrill. Stanford-Binet Intelligence Scale, 1972 ed. Iowa City: Houghton Mifflin, 1972.

Literature

Carroll, Lewis. *Alice's Adventures in Wonderland.* New York: New American Library, 1960.

Johnson, Crockett. *Harold and the Purple Crayon.* New York: Harper & Row, 1955.

Juster, Norton. *The Phantom Tollbooth.* New York: Random House, 1961.

Wilder, Thornton. *Our Town.* New York: Harper & Row, 1938.

CHAPTER 7

Works of Piaget

Piaget, Jean. *The Moral Judgment of the Child.* New York: The Free Press, 1965.

Literature

Barrie, James M. *Peter Pan.* New York: Charles Scribner, 1950.

Carroll, Lewis. *Alice's Adventures in Wonderland.* New York: New American Library, 1960.

De St. Exupéry, Antoine. *The Little Prince.* New York: Harcourt Brace, 1943.

Golding, William. *Lord of the Flies.* New York: G. P. Putnam's Sons, 1954.

Milne, A. A. *Winnie-the-Pooh.* New York: E. P. Dutton, 1926.

Twain, Mark. *The Adventures of Huckleberry Finn.* Boston: Riverside Editions, Houghton Mifflin, 1958.

CHAPTER 8

Works of Piaget

Piaget, Jean. *Science of Education and the Psychology of the Child.* New York: Viking Press, 1972, p. 162.

————. *The Language and Thought of the Child.* New York: Harcourt, Brace and World, 1926.

————. *The Grasp of Consciousness.* Cambridge, Mass.: Harvard University Press, 1976.

Related Readings

Almy, M. "New Views on Intellectual Development in Early Childhood Education." In Irene J. Athey and Duane O. Rubadeau, eds., *Educational Implications of Piaget's Theory*. Waltham, Mass.: Ginn-Blaisdell, 1970, pp. 61–75.

Ball, S., and G. A. Bogatz. "Reading with Television: An Evaluation of The Electric Company." Princeton, N.J.: Educational Testing Service, 1973.

Boyer, E. L. *Ready to Learn: A Mandate for the Nation*. Princeton, N.J.: The Carnegie Foundation for the Advancement of Teaching, 1991.

Bruner, J. S. "The Course of Cognitive Growth." *American Psychologist* 19 (1964): 1–15.

Friedrich, L. K., A. H. Stein, and E. Susman. "The Effects of Prosocial Television and Environmental Conditions on Preschool Children." Paper presented at American Psychological Association, Chicago, Ill., Sept. 1975.

Gelman, R., and C. R. Gallistel. *The Child's Understanding of Number*. Cambridge, Mass.: Harvard University Press, 1978.

Marsh, M. *Everything You Need to Know About the Information Highway*. Palo Alto, Calif.: Computer Learning Foundation, 1995.

Mermelstein, E., E. Carr, D. Mills, and J. Schwartz. "Training Techniques for the Concept of Conservation." In Irene J. Athey and Duane O. Rubadeau, eds., *Educational Implications of Piaget's Theory*. Waltham, Mass.: Ginn-Blaisdell, 1970, pp. 270–83.

Parents' Choice. Waban, MA 02168-0002. Phone (617) 965-5913.

Program Evaluation Measure (PEM). Baltimore City Public Schools—Office of Pupil and Program Monitoring and Appraisal, Baltimore, Md.

Singer, D. G., and J. L. Singer. "Family TV Viewing Habits and the Spontaneous Play of Preschool Children." *American Journal of Orthopsychiatry* 46, no. 3 (July 1976).

Singer, D. G., J. Caldeira, and J. L. Singer. "The Effects of Television Viewing and Predisposition to Imagination on the Language of Preschool Children." Paper presented at Eastern Psychological Association, April 1977.

———. *The House of Make-Believe: Play and the Developing Imagination.* Cambridge, Mass.: Harvard University Press, 1990.

Singer, J. L., and D. G. Singer. *"Barney & Friends" as Education and Entertainment. Series of Reports to Connecticut Public Television.* New Haven: Yale University, 1993, 1994, 1995.

Singer, D. G., J. L. Singer, and D. M. Zuckerman. *The Parent's Guide: Use TV to Your Child's Advantage.* Sarasota, Fla.: Acropolis South, 1995.

Source Books for Games and Exercises Related to Piaget's Theory

Durkin, L. L. *Special Times for Parents and Kids Together.* New York: Warner Books, 1987.

Isenberg, J. *Creative Expression and Play in the Early Childhood Curriculum.* Canada: Maxwell Macmillan, 1993.

Katz, S. A., and J. A. Thomas. *Teaching Creatively by Working the Word, Language, Music and Movement.* Boston: Allyn and Bacon, 1996.

Mayesky, M. *Creative Activities for Young Children.* Albany, N.Y.: Delmar Publishers, 1990.

Monighan-Nourot, P., B. Scales, J. Van Hoorn, and M. Almy. *Looking at Children's Play.* New York: Teachers College Press, 1987.

Rosenberg, H. S. *Creative Drama and Imagination: Transforming Ideas into Action.* New York: Holt, Rinehart and Winston, 1987.

Singer, D. G., and J. L. Singer. *Make Believe: Games and Activities to Foster Imaginative Play in Young Children.* Glenview, Ill.: Scott, Foresman and Company, 1985.

Zweiful, F. *The Make-Something Club.* New York: Viking, 1994.

Index